Don't Put a Period
Where God Put a Comma

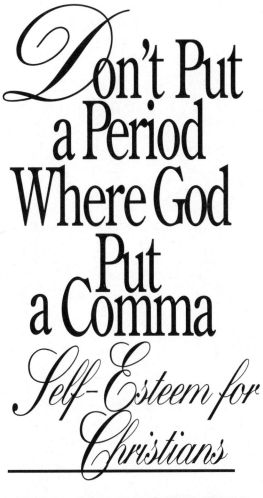

Don't Put a Period Where God Put a Comma

Self-Esteem for Christians

NELL W. MOHNEY

DIMENSIONS

FOR LIVING

NASHVILLE

DON'T PUT A PERIOD WHERE GOD PUT A COMMA
Self-Esteem for Christians

Copyright © 1993 by Dimensions for Living

This book is printed on acid-free, recycled paper.

Mohney, Nell.
    Don't put a period where God put a comma : self-esteem for Christians / Nell W. Mohney.
        p.   cm.
    ISBN 0-687-11061-0 (alk. paper)
    1. Self-esteem—Religious aspects—Christianity.   I. Title. II. Title: Do not put a period where God put a comma.
    BV4647.S43M65   1993
    248.4—dc20   93-359
                                                                    CIP

Unless otherwise noted, Scripture quotations are from the New Revised Standard Version Bible, Copyright 1989 by the Division of Christian Education of the National Council of the Churches of Christ in the USA. Used by permission.

Scripture quotations marked KJV are from the King James Version of the Bible.

95 96 97 98 99 00 01 02 — 10 9 8 7 6 5

MANUFACTURED IN THE UNITED STATES OF AMERICA

*T*o my grandchildren,

Ellen and Wesley Mohney,

whose parents

have enabled them to believe

in themselves and in their potential,

to love others easily,

and to love Christ purely.

$\mathscr{C}$ONTENTS

Contents

Contents

ACKNOWLEDGMENTS

My heartfelt appreciation is expressed to Mary Lee Simms—who has served as research assistant in finding, reading, and distilling information—and to all the persons who have allowed me to include their life experiences in this book.

INTRODUCTION

Perhaps one of the most important discoveries of the past fifty years is the growing awareness of how the self-image, the mental picture we each have of ourselves, affects all that we are and do. The self-image affects attitude and expectations as well as actions.

Through the centuries, the Bible has told us this in various ways. Proverbs 23:7 says, "As a man [person] thinketh in his heart, so is he" (KJV). In Matthew 22:36-39, we learn of the lawyer who comes to Jesus asking, "Teacher, which commandment in the law is the greatest?" Jesus replied: " 'You shall love the Lord your God with all your heart, and with all your soul, and with all your mind.' This is the greatest and first commandment. And a second is like it: 'You shall love your neighbor as yourself.' "

This book presents the biblical image of who we are and whose we are. We are created in the image of God (Genesis 1:27—"God created humankind in his image, in the image of God he created them; male and female he created them."); but because we have broken the image (Romans 3:23—"All have sinned and fall short of the glory of God"), we are redeemed by Christ (John 3:16—"For God so loved the world that he gave his only Son, so that everyone who believes in him may not perish but may have eternal life.") and empowered for living by the Holy Spirit (John 1:12—"But to all who received him, who believed in his name, he gave power to become children of God"; Acts 1:8—"But you will receive power when the Holy Spirit has come upon you . . .").

This is a powerful image and heritage! To claim it means to internalize the image in our thoughts, expectations, and attitudes and then to live it in the "nitty gritty" of everyday life. This book provides practical steps for the process. It also helps us see what interrupts and breaks the process—things such as fear, unresolved anger, worry, resentment, and perfectionism. To equip you for this process, questions for reflection appear throughout each chapter, and action-oriented exercises end each chapter to help you put the principles and suggestions within the chapters to work in your daily life. Choose the exercises that meet your unique needs—whether that be one, two, three, or all of them—and try them in the order best suited for *you*. The purpose here is to offer a wealth of suggestions for your choosing—not to overwhelm.

It is my desire to remind you that we put one "foot in heaven" when we come to faith and enter the kingdom of God, but we are Christians under construction. God hasn't finished with us yet. When I become discouraged with my progress, I remember Paul's words to the Philippians: "The one who began a good work among you will bring it to completion" (Philippians 1:6).

The Christian life is an exciting journey toward wholeness. Join me as we discover a few of its dimensions.

Don't Put a Period
Where God Put a Comma

CHAPTER ONE

A New Creation

*S*he looked as if she were in her early thirties. She was average height, average weight, average in every aspect of outward appearance, and yet she was totally appealing. Each person seated in the room waiting for the seminar to begin noticed her that day.

There was an aliveness about her. She exuded energy and interest, joy in being alive, and openness to others. Though I had heard that we all radiate our character and personality, I had never seen it as vividly as I did that day.

The quotations I had heard so often began to make sense to me: "What you are shouts so loudly in my ear, I cannot hear what you say" (Ralph Waldo Emerson); "The medium is the message" (Marshall McLuhan); "As a man [person] thinketh in his heart, so is he" (Proverbs 23:7 KJV); "We are not responsible for the face we are born with, but we are responsible for the face we die with" (E. Stanley Jones).

When the seminar ended, I invited the young woman— Kathy was her name—to join me for dinner. We talked for hours, and I learned that she had not always radiated such wholeness. In fact, she had grown up in a dysfunctional family where she was a victim of verbal abuse by her mother and of physical abuse by an alcoholic father. An only child, she grew up feeling lonely and rejected.

Since there was no relative living within two hundred miles of their small town and since her parents did not attend church, there was no one with whom to talk, no one who gave her affirmation. Though born with a happy, optimistic temperament, the constant abuse caused her to develop a self-image of unworthiness. As she described it, "I felt like a big zero."

Her naturally happy disposition soon turned into one of shy withdrawal. She desperately wanted to relate to other children, but she didn't know how. Without help or encouragement from home, her grades never reflected her intellectual ability. In fact, she was sure that some of her teachers considered her mentally slow.

The first door of opportunity for wholeness was opened by a girl who sat at the desk behind her in the sixth grade. The girl told Kathy that her Sunday school teacher had told each of the class members to invite someone to attend the class.

"Do you go to Sunday school and church?" the girl asked Kathy. "No, I don't," was the shy reply. "Do you want to meet me at the front of my church at 9:30 this Sunday?" asked the young disciple. "I'll ask my mother," said Kathy as her heart fairly jumped for joy.

Mrs. Parsons, the compassionate, loving sixth-grade Sunday school teacher then became, in Kathy's opinion, her guardian angel, and Kathy still thinks of Mrs. Parsons as such. Though she was a young woman at the time, Mrs. Parsons possessed great wisdom. She saw the children as individuals and wanted to help them become whole persons through Jesus Christ.

Mrs. Parsons took a special interest in Kathy, often inviting the girl into her home where the two of them had long talks. She told Kathy that God loved her and that Jesus' death on the cross shows us how much he loves us.

She helped Kathy learn to love herself and to discover her unique talents. When Kathy made good grades or participated in an activity at school or church, she knew she would receive an encouraging note from Mrs. Parsons. Kathy also learned relational skills as she worked with other children on classroom projects and participated with them in the first parties she had ever attended. Life became hopeful and exciting for the young girl.

Of eternal significance was the friendship Mrs. Parsons developed with Kathy's mother. In her own way, the victimized mother felt as alienated as her daughter. Through Mrs. Parsons, she learned of her daughter's needs and developed parenting skills as modeled by the Sunday school teacher. More important, it was Mrs. Parsons who led both mother and daughter to a heart-felt commitment to Christ and hence to a strong friendship with each other.

It was when she could finally forgive her father that Kathy experienced her greatest breakthrough to freedom. When we talked, her father had not yet come to faith but had been sober for five years and no longer abused her mother.

As we talked over dinner, Kathy told me that she believes the key to living happily was given by Jesus when he said: " 'You shall love the Lord your God with all your heart, and with all your soul, and with all your mind.' This is the greatest and first commandment. And a second is like it: 'You shall love your neighbor as yourself' " (Matthew 22:37-39). "Yet," she continued, "I am not sure that I could ever have loved God if Mrs. Parsons hadn't modeled his love for me and helped me to love myself."

"Has your self-image changed?" I asked as we sipped after-dinner coffee. "About 180 degrees," she replied. "The zero has changed to a number 10 with an exclamation point. I see myself as a person of great worth, not because of what I have done, but because of what God has done for me through Christ. To quote Mrs. Parsons: 'You are made in the image of God, redeemed by Christ, and empowered by the Holy Spirit.' "

It was the joyful empowerment that I saw in Kathy that day that motivated me to write this book on the importance of positive self-image and high self-esteem.

Like Kathy, we no longer have to live with feelings of loneliness, rejection, and unworthiness. Instead, as we receive God's love, we are able to perceive ourselves as "new creations"—persons full of potential and worthy of respect. When we learn to love ourselves, we can be open to others, see them as persons of worth, and be instruments through whom God's love is made visible.

CHAPTER TWO

A Christian Value System

$\mathscr{A}$fter we come to faith in Christ—become "a new creation"—we need a Christian value system by which to organize our lives. I once heard a story that symbolizes the very core of persons with a Christian value system.

Gorman Williams, a missionary from India, spoke in the chapel at Princeton University. He told of an experience that happened in 1945. He had purchased his ticket for a long-awaited furlough back to the United States. Then he heard of some Jews who had escaped from Germany and had come by boat to India, hoping to find refuge. The Indian government would not allow them to immigrate there but did grant permission for them to stay a short time in the lofts of buildings along the dock. They were living in cramped, inhumane conditions.

It was Christmas Eve when Williams heard about the Jews. He went immediately to the dock, entered the first building and called out: "Merry Christmas! What would you like for Christmas?" They replied: "We're Jewish." "I know," said Williams, "but what would you like for Christmas?" The weary Jews replied: "We would like some German pastries."

Selling his ticket to America, Williams purchased German pastries—lots and lots of them, large baskets full. As he told the story to the seminarians, one brash, judgmental young freshman stood and reprimanded the missionary: "You shouldn't have done that. They were not even Christians." "No, they weren't," quietly replied the missionary, "but I am."

A CORE COMMITMENT

The people who are making a strong, positive difference in our world today are those who have inner moorings, or an inner gyroscope that enables them to navigate the rapids of life with peace and confidence. They are not centered on themselves but are rooted and grounded in the God who created the universe and who, through Christ, offers eternal life to all who seek it.

> *Am I so rooted and grounded in faith that I am not pushed around by every circumstance of life?*

This core commitment determines their perception of the universe, of their fellow human beings, of relationships, and even of time. My observation is that they have learned to live fully in the "now" and to lean forward into the future, rather than reliving the past. They have an inner strength, and subsequently they exude the kind of confidence and hope that is appealingly contagious.

I believe that God is calling us to be God's people in the "now." Persons who insist on living in the past can't take advantage of opportunities for growth and service in the "now." All their energies are wasted in worry over old mistakes or fantasies as they relive former glories. The mental pictures these people carry are not ones of quiet, confident assurance but of fragmentation, unhappiness, and spiritual impotence.

When I think of people living in the past, I recall a humorous story about a Sunday school teacher and a group of children. The teacher was telling the children about Lot and his wife. She said, "Lot's wife looked back and turned into a pillar of salt." A seven-year-old boy raised his hand and said, "My momma looked back to see what we were doing in the back seat, and she turned into a telephone pole."

Then I think of the English schoolgirl who was taking an examination that included some biblical questions. One of them concerned Lot's wife. The child confused Lot's wife with the children of Israel in the wilderness who were led by a pillar of cloud by day and a pillar of fire by night. In response to the question "What happened to Lot's wife?" the child replied, "She turned into a pillar of salt by day and a ball of fire at night." Contemporary Christians don't turn into a pillar of salt by living in the past, but they do give evidence of having a negative self-image.

Dr. Stephen Covey emphasizes the importance of core commitment in his popular book, *The Seven Habits of Highly Effective People.* His book has been a *New York Times* best seller and has been studied by business and educational groups across the United States. Before Covey lists the seven habits, he says that no one can be truly effective unless his or her life is based not on techniques and personality skills but on never-changing principles. It seems to me that Dr. Covey gives a contemporary interpretation of Jesus' parable of building your house on rock rather than sand (Matthew 7:24-27). It is this kind of core commitment that allows us to live out the great commandment: " 'You shall love the Lord your God with all your heart, and with all your soul, and with all your mind.' And a second is like it: 'You shall love your neighbor as yourself' " (Matthew 22:37-39).

WHAT IS YOUR PICTURE OF YOURSELF?

Perhaps one of the greatest psychological discoveries of the past fifty years has been an understanding of how the mental picture we carry in our minds affects all that we do or think. If we are extremely fortunate, we are born with a happy temperament and into a home where parents, siblings, and later peers and teachers offer us acceptance and affirmation. A commitment to Christ validates this picture and allows us to see God's purposes for other people and the world.

If ours is a negative, limiting self-image, it sabotages our opportunities for personal fulfillment, inner peace, and service to others. Remember how Kathy was unable to use all of her mental abilities or reach out to others in warmth and caring until she was helped to receive a positive identity given by Christ—created in the image of God, redeemed by Christ, and empowered by the Holy Spirit.

If our self-image is negative, we often distort reality to fit the image. Dr. Maxwell Maltz, plastic surgeon and author of *Psycho-Cybernetics,* says that when he performs facial surgery that literally transforms a face, the patient will never see or accept the difference unless his or her mental self-picture corresponds to it. He tells of an attractive woman who came to his office. Her only unattractive facial feature was a large nose with a slight hump on it. The nose just didn't seem to belong with the otherwise delicate features. The woman told him that she had been unhappy most of her life because of her oversized nose.

Dr. Maltz performed the plastic surgery, and when the bandages were removed, Dr. Maltz was delighted to see that the new nose matched perfectly the woman's other facial features. Eagerly he held the mirror for the woman to see her new self. "Well, how do you like the new you?" he inquired. Staring directly into the mirror, the woman replied, "I don't see much difference." Despite successful surgery, this woman's mental picture of herself was that of an ugly, unappealing woman. That picture controlled her thoughts, attitudes, and actions.

If our self-image is strong-holding a belief that we are worthy, competent, growing persons with infinite potential, then we will not be held back by physical, emotional, or mental "blemishes" or handicaps, nor by an impoverished background. Henry Ford II was right on target when he said, "If you think you can, or if you think you can't, you are right."

One of the best examples we have of the power and importance of self-image is the life of W. Mitchell of Denver, Colorado. In 1960, W. Mitchell was a handsome, young man just out of the Marine Corps and happily settled as a radio announcer in Honolulu, Hawaii. He became involved, as did most American youths in the sixties, in politics. In 1968 he moved to the mainland to attend San Francisco State College and to work with the Robert Kennedy presidential campaign. One morning en route by motorcyle to the college, Mitchell was hit head on by a laundry truck. The lid to the gas tank popped off, the motorcycle exploded, and Mitchell was burned over 65 percent of his body. For two weeks, doctors at San Francisco General Hospital felt that he likely would not live.

Four months and several surgeries later, Mitchell went, at the invitation of his girlfriend's mother, to their home where he was cared for until he completed his rehabilitation and was able to function independently. A part of the rehabilitation was to learn to use the stubs that once had been his fingers. Perhaps the hardest thing to accept was the ridicule of strangers and the curious stares that people gave his twisted and scarred face. He still remembers going by a playground in his wheelchair and having the children call him a monster. Instead of hurrying past, he stopped and talked with the children, explaining that though he might look different on the outside since the accident, he was still the same on the inside—with the same feelings. Then he gave the children a statement that has become his creed and the subject of most of his speeches: "It is not what happens to you that is important, but how you react to what happens." What a learning experience for those children!

As soon as he was able, Mitchell got involved in radio, TV, and politics again. In 1971, he was elected Mayor of Crested Butte, Colorado. For the past four years, he has been a full-time professional speaker, becoming one of the most popular motivational speakers among the National Speakers Association's three thousand membership.

In a recent interview, I asked Mitchell what has helped him most to make such a tremendous comeback. Without hesitation, he answered, "The prayers of many people, the love and support of friends, and one statement from Earl Nightingale which I heard years earlier. The statement was simple, but powerful: 'Adversity introduces one to himself and helps him to discover resources yet untapped.' "

Then he added, "I learned anew that I am responsible for my life. Life is full of choices, and I have the power to choose my reactions. I, also, can choose not to live with self-imposed limitations." As I listened to W. Mitchell I realized that there is certainly no handicap of his spirit. It's not surprising that he has brought encouragement, hope, and inspiration to thousands of persons.

SELF-IMAGE FORMS EARLY IN LIFE

Self-image forms early in life as we see ourselves through the eyes of family and other significant persons in our lives. If they are perfectionists, overly strict, or unloving and critical, we grow up feeling unworthy and inadequate. To change that early conditioning, even with the help of God, is a long, arduous task. If during the early years the significant others in our lives are loving and affirming, we emerge from early childhood with feelings of self-worth and positive expectations for the future. Even if parents are caring and positive, a very sensitive child sometimes misreads the body language and develops a feeling of inferiority.

A Day of Freedom

In my own life I had an older sister who was really well behaved and smart. That is a powerful combination! My parents never once said, "We wish you could be like your sister," but I could see their pleasure in her high grades and her obedient behavior.

I began to feel inferior. As hard as I tried to be good, I seemed continuously to be getting into one escapade after another. I not only got into them, but I got caught in the middle of them. As for grades, I made As in all the subjects I was interested in, but Bs and Cs in the ones that didn't interest me. In comparison with my sister, I felt dumb and inferior. These feelings always result in resentment, anger, and even rebellion. I remember, as well as if it were yesterday, my decision to rebel. I was in the sixth grade and feeling that since I couldn't be like my sister, I would be as different from her as I could be. Though I didn't recognize it at the time, that was my declaration of independence.

My first act of rebellion was refusal to join the church. (I now find this amusing since I am a minister's wife!) My parents wanted me to join; my minister wanted me to join; I wanted to join; but I wouldn't do it. Often I have wondered if I ever would have accepted God's love and what he has done for me through Jesus Christ if my earthly father had not released me from a faulty self-image.

It happened on a day when I brought home two bad things from junior high school—a bad report card and a bad note from the principal. Instead of angrily demanding why I couldn't do better (which he must have been tempted to do many times), Dad said, "Let's go take a walk." As we walked, my father put his arm around me and said quietly, "Something has been troubling you. Do you want to tell me what it is?" I had wanted to tell someone for a long time, but no one had asked. So, I blurted out, "Daddy, I can't be like sister." "Oh, you are not supposed to be," he said emphatically. Then he held out his left hand, and I can still see it in my mind's eye. Taking the index finger of his right hand, he pointed to his left palm, saying: "Nell, God put a treasure in you. It's different from any treasure anyone else has. It is not like your sister's or your brother's or anyone else's. What your mother and I want to do is to help you discover your treasure." That day, my father set me free to be me! I no longer had to be in someone else's mold. Shortly thereafter, I came to faith in Jesus Christ gladly and willingly—not to please my parents or my minister, but out of a deep desire to follow Christ and to live my life in service for him.

So, my first step toward personal freedom came in the commitment of myself to faith in Jesus Christ. It was then that I accepted myself as a person of worth with untapped potential. I began to feel positive and hopeful about my future and deeply sure that I was not alone.

A Second Day of Freedom

After my father helped me to realize my uniqueness, and after I received my central freedom through faith in Christ, I still had to work through my perfectionism and my need to please others. When my husband, Ralph, asked me to marry him, I declined because of the faulty image I had of the role of a minister's wife. In the small church in which I grew up, the ministers' wives I had known could play the piano and sing, and they all wore large hats. That's what I thought a minister's wife should do. So, when Ralph asked me to marry him, I said, "I'm sorry, I can't."

"Don't you love me?" he asked. Quickly I replied, "Of course I love you, but I can't marry you; I can't play and sing." (I figured I could get a big hat!) Stunned and relieved by my irrational logic, Ralph burst into laughter. He said, "Nell, that's the silliest thing I've ever heard. If you love Christ and love me and love these people we are called to serve, God will give us a good ministry together."

I discovered that he was right. Yet, for the first year of marriage, I tried to be the "perfect minister's wife." Soon it became evident that there wasn't just one image of the role, there were as many images as there were church members. My second most freeing day came when I said and meant, "Lord, I want to be the finest person I can be for you, but I am not going to play to the grandstand any longer." It was another step in experiencing who I am and whose I am.

FROM SELF-IMAGE TO SELF-ESTEEM

As we have seen, self-image is the mental picture we have of ourselves. Self-esteem stems from self-image but includes how the picture has changed because of our life experiences. In other words, self-esteem is the reputation we give ourselves.

Dr. Nathaniel Branden, renowned psychotherapist and pioneer in the study of self-esteem and author of several books including *Honoring the Self* and *The Psychology of High Self-Esteem*, defines self-esteem as feeling competent to face life and being worthy of happiness. In a speech I heard him make, Dr. Branden said that life confronts us with many obstacles and challenges, and if we feel competent, we will maximize our opportunities for success. If, on the other hand, we have low self-esteem, we set low expectations and give up too quickly. Obviously, high self-esteem is a powerful motivator to set high goals, to persevere, and to achieve them. Low self-esteem is a motivator to set low goals and encourages lack of perseverance.

Do I feel confident about life and worthy of happiness? How is this evidenced in my behavior and my relationships?

Do I really believe in and have I claimed my Christian heritage—"created by God, redeemed by Christ, and empowered by the Holy Spirit"? Do the people who know me perceive me as a joyful, confident, and growing Christian?

SHOULD CHRISTIANS HAVE LOW SELF-ESTEEM?

One of the most loving, though passive, Christian women I have ever known was named Virginia. She also lived in one of the most destructive, dehumanizing circumstances I have ever encountered. When asked why she allowed such abuse, it was obvious she didn't feel worthy of respect or love. Fortunately, there is a thrilling story of how she and her family received Christian counseling, how she claimed her Christian heritage (made in the image of God, redeemed by Christ, and empowered by the Holy Spirit) and changed her self-image. It didn't happen overnight, but it has happened!

Actually it began on a terrible night when her husband, in an uncontrollable rage, beat Virginia and her two children until she feared for her life. In a moment of calm, she grabbed the car keys, picked up the children, ages two and four, and drove to a Safe House in a nearby town. Through the help of a competent, Christian counselor at the Safe House, she began to see some options available to her. She began to recognize that her own unhappy childhood caused her negative self-image, which allowed her to believe that she deserved such abuse. When the counselor convinced Virginia that staying in an abusive situation would be placing her children in jeopardy, not only for their lives but also for receiving the same negative self-images that Virginia and her husband had received, Virginia took action.

She knew that her husband needed help. He was a good man at heart who really loved his family, but he had never learned skills to handle his pent-up rage. When confronted, he agreed to go for counseling if Virginia would consider re-establishing their home after he received help. Through long months of counseling during which both came to faith in Christ, a new family was born. In addition, becoming active in a church gave them support and help from a network of new friends.

For the first time, Virginia began to understand the three dimensions of God's grace—prevenient, justifying, and sancti-fying. His prevenient grace surrounded her before she even knew how to come to faith. It gave her a sense of inner emptiness but a hope that there was a way out. His justifying grace took over when she recognized God's great love for her, made most evident by Jesus' death on the cross. When she accepted what Christ had done for her and invited him into her life as Savior and Lord, she received forgiveness and the assurance of her salvation. She became a new creation. God's sanctifying grace continues to work in her life through the presence of the Holy Spirit. His Spirit confronts, comforts, challenges, and empowers her to grow more and more into the likeness of Christ.

What is an area of my life that doesn't reflect the Lordship of Jesus Christ?

Many Christians have low self-esteem because they haven't yet accepted God's grace. Some even believe that because we are sinful and unworthy of God's grace, we should have low self-esteem. Such persons have a difficult time maintaining balance in their lives. Seeking to prove their worth, they have an inordinate need to please others. This is one of the reasons people become workaholics, "relationship-aholics" (so intent on maintaining a relationship that they fail to honor the self that God has given), or perfectionists. The pressure of trying to live with an inner conflict denies the real self. Trying to maintain a phony self-image can lead to fatigue and excesses such as overeating, alcohol and drug abuse, sexual promiscuity, as well as fragmentation, irritability, and uncontrollable temper.

As Christians we need to remember that we are made in the image of God ("made a little lower than the angels and crowned with honor and glory"), redeemed by Christ, and empowered by the Holy Spirit. That is a powerful heritage. We claim this heritage by affirming it; living in daily fellowship with Christ; practicing the holy habits of worship, prayer, and Bible study; being a part of the church, the Body of Christ; trusting God for the future; and serving him.

EXERCISES FOR DEVELOPING HIGH SELF-ESTEEM

1. Sit down alone in a quiet place and make a list of your assets. The list can include such things as a healthy body and a good mind, but should also focus on your unique talents—such as friendliness, a talent for singing, speaking, playing a musical instrument, writing, cooking, organizing, and so on. Take time to give God thanks for each of these gifts and celebrate them.

2. Sit down quietly with yourself and make a list of things you wish to change or improve in order to be the person you were created to be. This list might include things such as improving health and physical fitness (regular exercise, nutritional eating, learning to relax, losing weight); learning new skills; giving up a destructive habit or a bad attitude; building relationships with significant others in your life; settling your past; or taking time to grow spiritually.

A word of caution: don't do the above two exercises on the same day. It is so easy to focus on our weaknesses rather than build on our strengths. Take time to recognize and celebrate your strengths.

3. Choose one of your weaknesses and make an action plan for one week to work on it. For example, if you choose to lose weight and become more physically fit, you can make an appointment with a weight reduction group and/or an exercise program. Or you can decide to watch your fat intake, give up a dessert each day, and walk fifteen to thirty minutes a day. Write down your plan and follow it. Make faith and prayer an important part of your action plan.

4. As you begin to get mastery over one area, begin to work on another, but always keep balance and perspective. Remember that we are Christians under construction and that there is no instant wholeness.

God's sanctifying grace is at work in us. Our job is to cooperate with him, to live in fellowship with Christ, and to know that "the one who began a good work among you will complete it" (Philippians 1:6).

AFFIRMATIONS TO IMPROVE SELF-ESTEEM

The following affirmations have helped me tremendously as I have sought to move from a negative, pessimistic self-image to a confident self-image that encourages me to grow in competence and to become what God is calling me to be.

Say one or more of the following affirmations when you first awaken. They can also be used anytime when you are feeling inferior or inadequate.

1. I am created in the image of God, redeemed by Jesus Christ, and empowered by the Holy Spirit.
2. "I can do all things through [Christ] who strengthens me" (Philippians 4:13).
3. "If God be for us, who can be against us" (Romans 8:31).
4. I am a Christian under construction. God hasn't finished with me yet.
5. "The one who has begun a good work among you will complete it" (Philippians 1:6).
6. I am unique. I like myself and enjoy being me.
7. Today, I will treat everyone with whom I come in contact (including myself) with respect and appreciation.
8. I am capable and confident. (Remember to look people in the eye. Direct eye contact when speaking or listening is one of the most important nonverbal indicators of self-confidence.)
9. I enjoy smiling and I smile frequently. (A smile communicates in every language your acceptance of yourself and others.)
10. "This is the day that the LORD has made, let us rejoice and be glad in it" (Psalm 118:24).

CHAPTER THREE

Don't Put a Period Where God Put a Comma

Don't put a period where God put a comma." That wonderful quotation was given me by my friend, the Reverend Elton Jones. When I asked where he got it, he laughed and said, "From the Holy Spirit, by way of radio." Wherever he got it, it is a wonderful quotation and applicable to so much of life.

As we think back on that first Easter, we remember that most people who witnessed the crucifixion—Romans, Jews, and followers alike—believed that this was the end for Jesus. They put a period at 3:00 P.M. on that Friday, but God placed only a comma there. Sunday was coming, and there would be a resurrection.

Just recently, I talked with a couple who two years ago were remarried—to each other. Early in their first marriage there was great conflict based primarily upon the immaturity and selfishness of both and their lack of religious faith. In total disgust, they put a period on that relationship, or so they thought. But God had only placed a comma there. They each came to know God better, and he did a beautiful job of changing their perspectives and enlarging their understanding. Two years ago, they changed the period, which they called "divorce," into a comma, which they called "a second chance for a new beginning."

Another example comes from my own family. After years of alcoholism, my father and most of my family members put a period on my dad's life. Most of us didn't believe that he would ever stop drinking and even may have doubted God's power to change him, but God and my mother put a comma where he had placed a period. Through God's power and my mother's love, my dad lived the last twenty years of his life in sobriety.

THE PERIOD CAN BE ERASED

How many teachers and parents have put a period on the life of a difficult child? For the past two years I have had the privilege, under the auspices of the University of Tennessee, to speak throughout the state of Tennessee to conferences for foster parents. These courageous people are seeking to erase the period on the lives of neglected, abused children and place God's comma there. I never speak to these people without remembering a story I once heard about Miss Thompson and her three letters from Teddy Stallard.

Teddy had been a student in Miss Thompson's fifth grade. From the day he entered her classroom, she didn't like him. He was dirty, and his hair hung low over his ears. He had to hold it out of his eyes as he wrote his papers in class. (That was before it was fashionable to have long hair!)

By the end of the first week, she was aware that he was hopelessly behind the others academically. She began to withdraw from him and to determine that he would not be promoted to the sixth grade.

Then it was the day before the Christmas holidays began. Teachers always get several gifts at Christmas, but that year Miss Thompson's gifts seemed bigger and more elaborate than usual—that is, until she came to Teddy's. Its wrappings were a brown paper bag on which he had colored Christmas trees and red balls. It was stuck together with masking tape.

When she opened the bag, two items fell to her desk—a gaudy rhinestone bracelet with several stones missing and a small bottle of dime store cologne, half empty. The children began to snicker and whisper, and Miss Thompson wasn't sure she could look at Teddy. For the first time, she felt sympathy for the little boy.

"Isn't this lovely?" she asked as she placed the bracelet on her wrist and asked Teddy to fasten it. Then she put some cologne behind her ears and the girls lined up for a little dab behind their ears.

The children filed out of the room with shouts of "Merry Christmas." Teddy stayed behind and said shyly, "You smell just like my mom. Her bracelet looks real pretty on you, too. I am glad you like it."

When he left, Miss Thompson put her head in her hands and wept. She went to the office and checked his cumulative record. For the first and second grades the teachers had written: "Teddy shows promise by work and attitude but he has a poor home situation." Third grade: "Teddy is a pleasant boy, helpful but too serious. His mother passed away at the end of the year." Fourth grade: "Teddy is well behaved but is a slow learner. His father shows no interest in the boy."

After Christmas, Miss Thompson resolved to make up to Teddy what she had deliberately deprived him of—a teacher who cared. As a result, he did not have to repeat the fifth grade. In fact, his final average was among the highest in the class. He moved out of state that summer, and she didn't hear from him until seven years later when the first of three letters appeared.

The first told her that he was graduating second in his high school class. Four years later he wrote that he was graduating first in his class at a university. The final letter said, "Dear Miss Thompson, as of today, I am Theodore J. Stallard, M.D. I am going to be married in July, and I wanted to ask if you will come and sit where my mom would sit if she were here. I will have no family there, as Dad died last year. Sincerely, Teddy Stallard." Her reply was, "Dear Ted: Congratulations! You made it and you did it yourself! In spite of those like me and not because of us, this day has come for you. God bless you. I'll be at that wedding with bells on!"

Take a look at your own life. Are you putting a period where God has placed a comma? Are you limiting your potential by living in prisons of your own making? Look at the significant others in your life—members of your family, associates at work, friends. Are you limiting their achievements by low expectations? Don't put a period where God has placed a comma!

How am I limiting my God-given potential? By critical self talk? By fear of failure? By unwillingness to try something new? By unwillingness to be specific in listing expectations?

THE POWER OF EXPECTATION

I once read about a group of people who had experimented with expectations. There were six couples who were together for New Year's Eve. One man asked the group to experiment with his theory that our deep expectations help to determine what happens in our lives.

When they agreed, he suggested that each person present write on a three-by-five card what he or she deeply expected would happen in their lives during the coming year. They were to place the cards in an envelope, seal the envelope, and plan to open it the following New Year's Eve when they were all together again.

All except one man, who had died during the year, were present for dinner the following New Year's Eve. When it was time to open the envelope, they called on the widow to read what her husband had written. When she opened the envelope she gasped. Her husband had written: "If I am alive this time next year (both my father and my brother died during their forty-seventh year), I expect to. . . ." As the story unfolded and the others read their cards, there was such a "coincidence" between what they had expected and what had actually happened that I began to look seriously at my own life. Was I missing something that God had planned?

As I thought and prayed about the expectations experiment, I realized that God gave us the ability to imagine, to envision, and to dream—to dream God's dreams. So, one New Year's Eve many years ago, I wrote my first list of "great expectations." A doubting Thomas by nature, I entered rather tentatively into the experiment. I listed ten things that I really wanted, none of them material.

Most of my expectations that first year had to do with personal growth (physical, mental, emotional, and spiritual fitness), and relationships with my husband, our sons, and the faculty and student body of the college where my husband was serving as president.

Since I was such a skeptic, I added a postscript as a kind of test. I had wanted a small, magnifying mirror for applying makeup when I traveled. I had not been able to find one locally and because it wasn't very important, I'd never put in on a list of suggestions for birthday or Christmas.

In early March of that year, two months after I had written my first list of expectations, I accompanied my husband to an educational meeting in Boston. One morning I stayed in the hotel room while he went to a meeting. When he returned at noon, he brought me a present from the hotel gift shop. When I opened it, I was stunned to find the travel mirror—the small postscript that I had added to my list of expectations. Before I could even say "thank you," I asked, "Why did you happen to choose this?" "Don't you like it?" Ralph asked. "I really like it, but have I ever mentioned that I wanted it?" I was probing for logical explanations. "No. You've never mentioned it," he conceded. "Then, why did you buy it?" I persisted. By this time he was wondering why he had and wishing he hadn't. In exasperation, he replied, "I don't know, but when I saw it I thought, that's something Nell would like."

As I have laughingly told this incident, I've always said, "That experience frightened me so that I looked carefully at the other ten things on the list so I would be sure I really wanted them."

Each year since then, I have listed my great expectations. As I write each one, I give it two tests. First, is there anything in this expectation that will hurt me or anyone else? Second, is there anything in my desire that is not in keeping with God's will and purpose? If the expectation passes both tests, I toss it heavenward and make it a part of my thoughts and prayers just before I go to sleep at night and when I awaken each morning.

Not all my expectations have become reality, but so many have that it has confirmed for me the power of expectations. As I look back over the years and note some of the dreams that have been realized, I feel like praying the prayer that the late Gert Behanna made so famous: "Lord, I ain't what I ought to be; I ain't what I'd like to be; and I ain't what I'm going to be, but thank God I ain't what I used to be!"

One year one of my great expectations was, "It is my deep desire to host a television program in which I interview people about their faith." Our church had just completed a building program that included a television studio. Our Sunday worship services were being telecast, and some of us envisioned originating weekday programming in the studio. I am sure that this had influenced my expectations.

But God had a little different twist to that dream. One week from the day I had written the dream, the executive vice president of a local newspaper called to say, "Nell, we would like to invite you to write a weekly Sunday feature article in which you interview someone about their faith"—the very words I had written. I was stunned into silence. Finally, she asked, "Nell, are you there?" When I told her the story, she said, "It is an answer to prayer, an open door. Walk through it." A week later I walked into her office talking like Moses. I told her all the reasons I couldn't possibly do what she asked—I couldn't write well, I didn't know that many people, I didn't have time, and so on. I walked out of her office thanking her for the opportunity. My life continues to be enriched because of that opportunity.

Who are the people in my life I am limiting through low expectations, criticism, sarcasm, gossip, or by ignoring them? (List these persons by name, ask God's forgiveness of your low expectations, and make a plan of action whereby you can take some positive steps to correct the negative influences.)

Now, years later, my articles still appear in two area newspapers.

If you allow yourself to think carefully about those persons who have believed in you even when you didn't believe in yourself, the people who come to mind may surprise you. Only recently when I spoke at the International Women's Conference at the Crystal Cathedral in Garden Grove, California, did I realize how much a junior high counselor in our church had done for me.

As a youth I was terrified at the thought of speaking in front of people. So, the youth counselor at my church would come to the church early on Sunday evening and practice with me when I had a part on the evening's youth program. Always she would say, "You can do it, Nell. You can do it."

Through the years I have spoken to all kinds of groups without apprehension and without a thought of that junior high counselor. Then last fall when I arose to speak to that large audience in the Crystal Cathedral, I suddenly had butterflies in my stomach for the first time in years. The face of that junior high counselor flashed into my mind and her encouraging words—"You can do it, Nell, you can do it"—calmed and soothed my spirit.

OUR EXPECTATIONS INFLUENCE OTHERS

Most of us have heard and marveled at some version of the San Francisco Bay experiment. According to the report, this double-blind experiment originated in the mind of the superintendent of the Bay Area schools. He called in two teachers and explained that because they were unusually talented teachers, he was giving them each a class of gifted children. He wanted to see what would happen when gifted teachers taught only gifted students for a year.

The experiment had to be kept secret. Only the three of them would know. They must not mention this to friends, their students, or parents of the students. At the end of the year, the results were truly amazing. All of the students had progressed remarkably. The superintendent then admitted to the teachers that they had not had gifted children in their classes. In fact, the children had been chosen at random. The teachers, though surprised, must have felt it was their exceptional teaching skills. Then he admitted that their names had been drawn out of a hat. It was a double-blind experiment. The only differential had been the high expectations in the minds of the teachers.

Low expectations are even more powerful. One of the unforgettable films released by the Encyclopedia Britannica of Chicago is entitled *Cipher in the Snow*. It is the story of a shy, sensitive boy whose verbally abusive step-father criticized and ridiculed the boy's every expressed thought and action. His passive, victimized mother had no ego strength left for affirming her son. Without relational skills and withdrawing more and more, the boy had no friends, no one to notice or care. One snowy day as he rode the bus to school, he told the driver to stop and let him off the bus. At the bottom of the steps, the boy collapsed in the snow and was dead on arrival at the hospital.

The teacher who was asked to speak at the boy's funeral service was tormented by the thought that the boy had been in one of his classes and yet he had no memory of the child. To the principal the teacher reported: "That boy died of a broken heart. He was only a cipher in the snow." What a challenge to all of us to honor the self in each person we meet through affirmation and the power of expectation.

> **What skills of affirmation do I most need to develop and practice? Appreciation? Listening? Giving honest compliments? Encouragement? Praying for others?**

EXERCISES FOR DEVELOPING THE SKILL
OF EXPECTATION

1. Set aside some time right now to begin a list of your "great expectations" for the remainder of the year. After this, you can begin this exercise on New Year's Eve or the first of January.

A. You may want to consider listing your expectations in four categories: personal growth—physically, mentally, emotionally, spiritually; professional growth; relationships; financial goals.

B. Be sure that these expectations are something that you truly desire. Remember James Montgomery's powerful words: "Prayer is the soul's sincere desire, unuttered or expressed."

C. Let the expectations pass the test of whether or not they will hurt you or someone else and whether or not they are in keeping with God's will and purposes. You might like to devise additional tests that are relevant for your situation.

D. Use your God-given talent of envisioning—using your imagination to visualize—to see yourself as having fulfilled the expectations. A good time to do this is just before you go to sleep and when you first awaken in the morning. Your subconscious mind is more open then, and your conscious mind less cluttered. It is then that the Holy Spirit works directly with the very core of your being.

2. Begin to observe and monitor your expectations of people who are close to you—spouse, children, parents, sister, brother, in-laws, co-workers. Are you limiting their achievements by low expectations?

3. Become more aware and appreciative of those persons who have believed in you even when you didn't believe in yourself as well as those who are currently bringing out the best in you. List them by name and list the skills they are using. Then, thank God gratefully for each of them.

CHAPTER FOUR

A Different You, Inside and Out

There is a new you coming every day" was the opening line of a jingle used in advertising by the American Dairy Association several years ago. It was based on the theory that new cells are born in our bodies every day, and that over a seven-year period we get completely new bodies, except for the enamel on our teeth. Every time I heard that jingle I found myself hoping that I would get a better looking body the next time around!

Whether we like it or not, our outer appearance helps determine how others perceive us, and hence how we picture ourselves. Social scientists say that when someone meets you for the first time, forty thousand impulses are mobilized in his or her mind as he or she scans such things as your personal appearance, facial expressions, body movement, tone of voice, color of skin, age, gender, and finally what you say.

He or she filters this information through the circumstances surrounding the meeting, the other person's self-image that day (the way he or she feels) and his or her expectations that were obtained through past experiences—what they had heard and read and their own prejudices. Social scientists suggest that 56 percent of the information others receive comes from body movement, eye contact, and facial expressions; 37 percent from tone of voice; and only 7 percent from what you say.

All of this indicates that the outer you houses the real you—the eternal you. These need to be blended together to reflect who we are—faithful disciples of Jesus Christ.

TAKE CARE OF YOUR BODY HOUSE

Certainly, you won't look very radiant or joyful if your body is not fit, or if your back or feet are hurting. We need to remember that our bodies are the temples of God (I Corinthians 6:19), and that our entire beings should be integrated, not fragmented. The physical affects the mental and spiritual parts of us. We need to keep physically fit, and take care of our body houses.

> *In what ways am I not using my body as the temple of God? (List each and suggest an action you will take to correct it.)*

Once when I was visiting a friend, her four-year-old daughter came in crying. "What's wrong?" asked the mother solicitously. "I fell off my big wheels," the little girl said between sobs. The mother pulled the little girl close to her and asked, "Are you hurt?" I was startled by the child's reply: "I am not hurt, but my body house is," she said, pointing to a scrape on her right leg.

After she was comforted and went outside, I asked my friend what the child meant by her reply. The mother explained: "Once when she was three, we were driving past a cemetery and Robin asked what it was. Realizing that small children have difficulty with abstract ideas, I tried to make the experience of death more understandable. So, I said, 'We all live in body houses and sometimes these body houses get hurt or old and then they have to be put here, but the real you goes on living with God.' Then I illustrated by saying, 'If I pinch you, it will hurt your body house, but it won't hurt you. If I make you sad or hurt your feelings, it will hurt you, but it won't hurt your body house.' "

So, that day, when asked if she were hurt, the little girl replied, "I'm not hurt, but my body house is." It occurred to me that many body houses have been taken to the cemetery long before necessary because the owners filled their arteries with fat, their lungs with nicotine, their livers with alcohol, and their stomachs with junk food. Eating nutritionally and keeping our body houses in world-class condition are vitally important. To do this, we must exercise. Bodies were not created to be sedentary but to be actively used. We need to keep those muscles moving. Unless we are ill, we all should exercise as long as we live. Gerontologists tell us that exercise and social involvement help to keep our brains stimulated as we get older.

Know Your Limitations

Of course, we can't do the same exercises at eighty years of age that we did at fifteen. We should know our limitations. I heard of a woman who really dreaded her husband's retirement. When asked why, she said, "He has never done anything that required physical exertion. He has never played golf, mowed the lawn, or washed the windows. When he retires, he will sit in his easy chair and expect me to bring him food."

Two weeks after he retired, he surprised her completely when he came in and said, "Martha, I went down to the Y and joined a class today." "Good! What is it?" she asked. "Wrestling," he answered nonchalantly. "Wrestling?" she shrieked. "You will be killed!"

Two weeks after that, he stunned her with this announcement: "Martha, I signed up for the wrestling tournament. I am going to wrestle Friday night." "Please don't do it," she begged. "They will bring you in bloody and beaten. I refuse to go watch." Friday night came. He went out to wrestle, and she stayed home to worry. At about 10:00 P.M., as she predicted, two men came helping him in. He was bloody and beaten, but before she could say anything like "I told you so," he said, "Don't say a word, Martha. This is not the worst of it. I won tonight. I have to fight tomorrow night!" Certainly as we get older, we need to know our limitations.

YOUR FACE CAN SAY YES

Another important aspect of outward appearance is facial expression. Though personal grooming is helpful, the most important thing you will ever wear is the expression on your face. It has been said that the face is a window to the soul. How we feel inside is reflected on our faces.

I have heard a story told about Thomas Jefferson before he became President. He was waiting in a line on horseback to ford a stream. He noticed a man standing on the bank looking as if he would like to ride across. Yet, five people went across the stream, and it was only when Jefferson rode up to the water that the man asked for a ride. Jefferson, of course, granted the man's request, but on the way over he said to his passenger, "I am pleased to give you a ride across the stream, but I noticed that you allowed five persons to go across without asking to ride with them. Why?" The man replied, "Some people's faces say yes and some people's faces say no."

When our sons were in elementary school, I was den leader for a Cub Scout group, which met in our basement every Wednesday afternoon. One Wednesday I took those little boys out to the airport to see a display of Confederate money. Since the guide was there to explain what they were seeing, I paid little attention to them. In fact, I was preoccupied with all the things I had to do in preparation for a women's meeting being held in our home that evening. When we were driving home, one of the Cub Scouts said to me, "Mrs.

Is my face reflecting my growing level of self-esteem and the joy of being a Christian? (During the day, occasionally look in a mirror to see what your face is saying to others.)

Mohney, are you mad at us?" Startled, I replied, "Oh no, I'm not angry. Why did you think that?" "Well, I didn't think that, but Jimmy did, and I told him that you had probably just eaten something that had upset your stomach." Since that day, I have looked carefully in the mirror each morning to see if I appear to have an upset stomach!

Since so much communication comes nonverbally, if we want others to perceive us as strong and caring, we need to cultivate faces that are kind, that smile, that say yes. Dr. E. Stanley Jones, missionary to India and evangelist to America, once said, "You are not responsible for the face you were born with, but you are responsible for the face you die with."

STRESS WITHOUT DISTRESS

Perhaps one of the most influential factors in how we feel and look, inside and out, is stress.

Have you ever had the Monday morning blahs seven days a week? Have you ever felt overwhelmed, frustrated, fragmented? Have you ever felt burned out or that you needed your spiritual batteries recharged?

All of us have felt like this at times. If, however, you are feeling this way rather consistently, you may be suffering from poor self-image and lack of spiritual grounding. Learning to deal with stress without distress is a top priority. You will never become whole in Jesus Christ if your system is on overload from debilitating stress.

Have I been aware of the difference between eustress (stress that motivates me) and distress (stress that overloads my system and debilitates me)?

Learning to relax is essential if we are to live successfully in the pressures of a fast-paced world. Life is full of stress. Some stress is good. This is called *eustress*. If we didn't have a certain amount of this kind of stress we would all be like soft, squishy marshmallows. I like the story of the mother who came in for the third time to try to get her son out of bed. This time she yanked the covers back and said with a commanding voice, "Now get out of that bed or you will be late for Sunday school and church." Sleepily he asked, "Give me three reasons why I have to go." "First," she replied, "it's Sunday; second, you are thirty-nine years old; third, you are the minister." That minister needed the eustress provided by his mother!

Then there is bad stress, called *distress*. Distress occurs when our systems are overloaded with pressures. To combat distress we need to learn to relax our bodies, to relax our minds, and to develop a calm center within. We need to exercise and to make time for family, friends, and fun. We also need to learn to laugh often and pray daily.

A recent scientific study of the brain indicates that two things release endorphins in our brains to create a sense of well-being. Those two things are laughter and prayer, or meditation. The late Dr. Norman Cousins in his book *Anatomy of an Illness* tells us that hearty laughter certainly aids in the healing of the body. Through the centuries, persons of faith have demonstrated the value of prayer in bringing integration and wholeness to their personalities.

In what one area of my life do I need most to take action to reduce or eliminate stress? (Most likely, one area more than any other is causing you debilitating stress. Isolate that area, plan your action, and then just do it. It was Lao-tzu who said: "The journey of a thousand miles must begin with a single step.")

Each morning as you dress, let a series of happy thoughts run through your mind. Remember a kindness expressed to you recently. Let gratitude permeate your spirit. It was Nehemiah who reminded us: "The joy of the LORD is your strength" (Nehemiah 8:10).

EXERCISES FOR REDUCING HARMFUL STRESS

1. Plan a suitable exercise program and then work your plan. The temptation is to say, "I don't have time." Actually, you don't have time *not* to exercise. A longer, less stressful, happier life is motivation enough to set aside thirty minutes three days a week for exercise. If you can exercise five times a week, or three times a week for one hour, you will be that much better off. Physical fitness experts say that you need three types of exercise: aerobic, stretching, and calisthenics.

A. Aerobic exercise develops cardiovascular efficiency (the ability of the heart to pump blood through your body) and produces endurance. Aerobic exercise includes such things as jogging, walking, biking, cross-country skiing, and swimming.

B. Stretching exercises, which can be done when you get out of bed each morning, will improve your flexibility. These help loosen and warm the muscles for more strenuous exercise. They also help to dissipate lactic acid so that you won't feel sore and stiff.

C. Simple calisthenics or exercising with weights will provide strength. If you are involved with physical labor or athletics, these are especially important. If your lifestyle is sendentary, you will need more aerobic exercise.

2. Eat nutritionally—nutritionists tell us that our diet drastically affects the way we feel about ourselves. Diet affects not only our weight, but our energy levels, our mood swings, and our ability to throw off disease.

A. Determine to eat food high in fiber, low in fat, sodium, and sugar.

B. Keep your weight within five pounds of your ideal weight. (Ask your physician for a chart providing this information.)

C. Remember that after thirty-five years of age, we can lower our caloric intake.

3. Get sufficient rest and sleep.

4. Have a physical examination annually.

5. Exercise control over the number of stresses you are experiencing. For example, if you are going through a divorce or the death of a loved one, don't voluntarily take on a job change, a move to a new location, or have a confrontation that may end a friendship.

6. Learn to say no without feeling guilty. This is particularly important for persons with low self-esteem because of their need to please others. Learning to say no involves establishing priorities and setting goals for a year at a time. Then you know what you can and cannot do. Being organized does not mean being rigid. There are times when you have to put priorities aside for something of greater importance. For example, your spouse, your children, or your boss may need your time right away, and you need to respond. That's being flexible, but it is not the kind of flexibility seen in a reed that bends before every wind that blows. You decide to change your priorities. You are still in charge.

7. Don't procrastinate. Meet your problems head on. Dreading a situation can cause much more stress than dealing with a problem.

A man told me once that he keeps a vase of thorns on his desk to remind him how to handle a problem. "If you touch it tentatively, it will prick you," he said, "but if you grab the whole thistle, it will crush and not hurt a bit."

8. Take mini-vacations. When things are fast and furious at home, take two minutes and close your eyes, relax

your body, and in your imagination go to a spot that is very peaceful to you. Soon, your mind will be calm and your stress level will be lower. Remember that ships don't come in on rough waters. You need to become calm in order to think clearly.

9. Learn to laugh easily. My observation is that many Christians are too intense, too nervous, too uptight. They need to see life in a larger perspective and realize that ultimately they are not in charge of the universe. God is. This does not mean that we shouldn't be proactive or take responsibility for our lives. It means that we act in trustful obedience to God and leave the results with God.

One of the best ways to do this is to learn to laugh easily. Laugh at yourself; laugh at things that you cannot change; train yourself to see humor all around you. It will not only enable you to enjoy life more, but it will enable you to be healthier.

10. Keep a healthy balance in your life—physically, mentally, emotionally, socially, and spiritually. Also, keep the balance between home and career.

11. Develop a career or avocation that is fulfilling.

12. Try new experiences that will add freshness to life.

13. Establish a few close relationships including family and non-family members that are characterized by acceptance and trust. In his book *Future Shock*, Alvin Toffler calls these "stability zones." Then devote time and energy to nurture these relationships.

14. Learn sound financial management. Many people are robbed of inner peace through worry over finances. A friend of mine described heaven as living under your income by $50.00 each month and hell by living over it

by $50.00 each month. That same man told me that in counseling young couples whose marriages are adrift from overspending, he often counsels, "cut up your credit cards." Of course, establishing credit is important but living beyond your means will take you out of the driver's seat of your life. Take a course, read a book, consult an expert, but learn financial management if you want good self-esteem.

15. Learn to delegate. If you are a parent, teach children to take over household responsibilities as soon as possible. If you are in the work force, learn to delegate some of your responsibilities.

16. Make a list of all the things that bother you and write beside each what action you will take. If you can't do anything to change a situation, such as a job, you still have three choices: accept it, continue to be frustrated and angry, leave the situation. Remember the prayer attributed to Reinhold Niebuhr:

> God grant me the serenity to accept the things I cannot change, the courage to change the things I can, and the wisdom to know the difference.

17. The most successful method of handling stress is meditation and prayer. Quiet prayer can slow your heart and respiratory rates, lower your blood pressure, clear your thinking, release anxiety, and help you sleep better.

Isaiah, a very wise man and prophet, knew this thousands of years ago. He wrote:

> Those who wait for the LORD shall renew their strength,
>   they shall mount up with wings like eagles,
> they shall run and not be weary,
>   they shall walk and not faint. (Isaiah 40:31)

CHAPTER FIVE

You May Not Be What You Think You Are; but What You Think, You Are

Your self-image is vastly affected by your conscious thoughts. Recently, a man who is known for being unhappy, opinionated, and pessimistic revealed the source of his unhappiness when he declared, "It doesn't matter what you think or believe, it's what you do that is important." Of course, it matters what you think! Thoughts are living entities. When consistently held they become attitudes. Then they become congealed convictions—the outer expression of our inner thoughts. It was the English author Samuel Smiles who in 1887 wrote: "Sow a thought, reap an action; sow an action, reap a habit; sow a habit, reap a character; sow a character, reap a destiny."

Philosophers, psychologists, teachers, and religious leaders have disagreed about many things through the years, but they all seem to be in agreement about the importance of thoughts. They use six words as the determinative difference between success and failure: "You become what you think about."

Throughout history many individuals have eloquently expressed the power of a person's thoughts. Marcus Aurelius, the great Roman emperor, said, "The world in which we live is determined by our thoughts." William Shakespeare wrote,

"Our doubts are traitors, /And make us lose the good we oft might win, /By fearing to attempt." In our own country the beloved author and philosopher Ralph Waldo Emerson wrote, "A person is what he or she thinks about all day long." Harvard sociologist and psychologist, William James, declared, "The greatest discovery of my generation is that human beings can alter their lives by altering their attitude of mind."

ATTITUDES ARE MORE IMPORTANT THAN FACTS

Thoughts that are consistently held and nurtured become attitudes. These attitudes are the powerful forces that mold and shape our very lives.

Charles Swindoll, a well-known Christian author and minister, wrote:

> The longer I live, the more I realize the importance of attitude on life. To me, attitude is more important than facts. It is more important than the past, than education, than money, than circumstances, than failures, than successes, than what other people say or do. It is more important than parents, giftedness or skill. It will make or break a company, a church, a home.
>
> The remarkable thing is we have a choice every day regarding the attitudes we will embrace that day. We cannot change our past; we cannot change the fact that people will act in certain ways; we cannot change the inevitable. The only thing we can do is play on the one string we have, and that is our attitude. I'm convinced that life is ten percent what happens to us and ninety percent how we react to it. We are in charge of our thoughts and attitudes.

The late Earl Nightingale, well-known motivational speaker, illustrated in a speech to business and professional people how attitudes affect our lives. He said that the mind is somewhat like an acre of land on which a farmer might plant a crop. He can plant a good crop, like corn, or a deadly poison, like nightshade. The land doesn't care what we plant, but will give us back in abundance what we plant.

Mr. Nightingale suggested that the mind, though far more creative and complex than the fallow land, is similar in that what we put in it, we get out. If we sow negative or evil thoughts, we will reap negative or evil results. If we sow positive or constructive thoughts, we will reap positive or constructive results.

The Bible certainly confirms this belief in numerous passages. Here are just a few examples:

As a man [person] thinketh in his heart, so is he. (Proverbs 23:7 KJV)

You reap whatever you sow. (Galatians 6:7)

Whatever is true, whatever is honorable, whatever is just, whatever is pure, whatever is pleasing, whatever is commendable, if there is any excellence and if there is anything worthy of praise, think about these things. (Philippians 4:8)

FOUR IMPORTANT ATTITUDES

Four important attitudes that will keep us open to the leadership of Christ in our lives are gratitude, magnanimity, thinking positively, and compassion. Let's look at each of these attitudes.

Gratitude seems to open your heart to life, to others, and to God. Ingratitude snaps it shut. I learned something of the power of gratitude following the death of our oldest son, Rick, who had just turned twenty and was a student at a local university. Rick was critically injured and died ten days later. It was such a traumatic experience that I had a very difficult time overcoming my grief. Each night when I went to bed, I felt as if there were a terrible black cloud hanging over my head. When I awakened the following morning, the cloud was still there. Though I never once blamed God for the accident and though I prayed regularly, I still was having problems handling my grief.

One of the things that helped me was to reread Paul's words to the Thessalonians: "Give thanks in all circumstances; for this is the will of God in Christ Jesus for you" (I Thessalonians 5:18). In that passage Paul did not say "*for* all circumstances give thanks." He didn't suggest that I give thanks that our son had died, but that in the midst of tragedy I should give thanks.

That simple statement transformed my perspective. Each morning before I got out of bed to take exercise and have a quiet time, I conditioned my mind with gratitude. Instead of focusing on what I had lost, I focused on what I still had. For example, upon awakening I would say something like, "Thank you, God, for your love made evident in Jesus Christ. Thank you for a husband who loves me. Thank you that we have another son. Thank you that we had Rick for twenty years and for our happy memories. Thank you for friends, a job to occupy my mind during much of each day, and a church that is truly the body of Christ." Each day I could feel my grief lifting.

That morning exercise of gratitude was so life changing that I continue it to this day. On the rare occasions when I oversleep and don't take time to "count my blessings," I find myself irritable and impatient with others.

My observation is that grateful people never take life for granted. They see life as a privilege, not a right. Grateful people are humble people. Humility, according to Phillips Brooks, a great nineteenth-century preacher, is "not stooping so that you are lower than yourself, but raising yourself to your full height beside a higher nature so that your smallness may be seen." In other words, humility is realizing that God is your source.

Gratitude also is expressed in acts of appreciation. Small expressions of appreciation—even as small as a simple thank-you note—can enrich and change the climate of a marriage; a friendship; a parent-child relationship; or an office, church, or volunteer organization.

The second important attitude is magnanimity—being generous instead of petty. You need to see every person as a child of God, a person of worth, even if you don't agree with or like him or her.

As a young person, I attended a World Conference of Christian Youth in Oslo, Norway. When we registered we were informed that we could not room with anyone from our own nation. That really frightened me because I had been "exposed" to French in high school and Spanish in college but spoke neither fluently. The thought of not being able to speak for two whole weeks bothered me even more.

When I went to my dormitory room, there were girls from several other nations who had already arrived. The girl in the bed just beside mine was from Germany. Thinking she might know French, I said, *"Parlez-vous français?"* She shook her head "No." Then she tried German and I shook my head. I tried Spanish and she shook her head. Finally, she asked, "Why don't we just use English?" I discovered that everyone in my room except one spoke English fluently. I learned so much from my association with those international students. We didn't look alike; we didn't wear the same kind of clothes. Even our toothbrushes were different. But we all laughed about the same things and were deeply moved by the same things. In addition, we were all Christians.

On the last night of the conference, we were asked to wear our native dress and sit under our national flag. The Bishop of Oslo led our worship by inviting us to stand and pray together the Lord's Prayer, using our own language or dialect. Later, it was announced that we had used 122 languages or dialects as we prayed, "Our Father who art in heaven.

> *Are the four important attitudes—gratitude, magnanimity, positive thinking, and compassion—a part of my daily living? If not, which attitude do I most need to work on?*

..." That night I joined the human race. Up to that time, I had been a white American from a provincial section of North Carolina. That night I began to see people as people—*God's* people.

The third important attitude is being positive instead of being negative. One of the most positive people I have ever known was Dr. E. Stanley Jones, whose books have had a powerful impact on the spiritual lives of millions of Christians around the world. As a young person, I considered Dr. Jones to be my spiritual mentor through his books. Later in life I had the opportunity to meet Dr. Jones when he accepted an invitation to preach in our church for a week and be a guest in our home. That experience was a "shining hour" in my spiritual journey.

E. Stanley Jones was positive because he truly believed that "Jesus is Lord," and he lived his life under the Lordship of Christ. His positive faith affected every area of his life—his health, his mental acumen, his time management, his relationships, and his availability to Christ. During that week I was painfully aware that at seventy-nine years of age he could outwalk me at thirty-two.

Dr. Jones believed that positive attitudes enhance physical healing. He certainly proved this when he suffered a crippling stroke at eighty-nine. Even though the paralysis persisted, he maintained a positive attitude rooted in his unassailable trust in Jesus Christ. He prayed and asked people around the world to pray that he would walk again. An around-the-clock vigil was arranged. When he awakened from sleep, either day or night, he insisted that the attending nurse repeat this energizing affirmation: "In the name of Jesus of Nazareth, rise and walk."

During his five-month stay in a Boston hospital, Dr. Jones used a tape recorder to chart his progress back to normalcy of speech. Then he began to dictate a book that was entitled *The Divine Yes*. The title certainly described his philosophy of life. He sought the "Divine Yes" for guidance and strategy for ministry. As he placed himself under the Lordship of Christ, he received the "Divine Yes" to use his unlimited potential. During his hospital stay, he wrote, "I haven't had a blue moment yet!"

Taken to the Himalayas in India to further recuperate, he continued in his positive response to the "Divine Yes" and was finally able to walk again and resume his preaching. He continued living and preaching victoriously until he moved from the earthly to the heavenly dimension of life.

The fourth important attitude is compassion—the ability to feel with others. It is the attribute that our Lord modeled so beautifully in his earthly existence. It was also modeled for me by a nine-year-old girl on the Sunday following our son's funeral service.

Rick's service had been on the previous Sunday, so our family members had returned home, our younger son had returned to college, and my husband was in the pulpit. I had to walk into church alone on that Sunday. It is one of the hardest things I have ever had to do, but I knew that postponing it would only make it harder.

That morning when I walked to the pew where Rick and I usually sat, there was a vacant seat beside me. Almost before I was seated, the nine-year-old girl left her parents, sat down beside me, and with the most disarming smile, simply patted my hand and said, "Mrs. Mohney, I love you." I knew what she was saying—"Mrs. Mohney, I know how you must feel this morning, and I'm sorry." All my carefully mustered control melted like ice in the sun. But I never shall forget that act of compassion or the touch of her small hand. Yes, as Christians we need to develop and express the attitude of compassionate caring.

THREE DEADLY ATTITUDES

Just as there are attitudes that will keep us open to the leadership of Christ in our lives, so also there are attitudes that will kill our spirits and prevent us from being receptive to Christ.

The first deadly attitude is playing the blame game. People with self-esteem that is rooted in the tremendous resources of God within, usually are proactive. They take responsibility for their own lives and don't waste time or energy blaming others. Life is not a bed of roses for any of us. Jesus told us, "In the world you face persecution. But take courage; I have conquered the world" (John 16:33).

When bad things happen to some people, they look for someone to blame—parents, boss, spouse, government leaders, even God. Some people choose an ethnic, religious, or political group as their scapegoat. This attitude of blame lowers self-esteem; leads to rejection, bitterness, and cynicism; and should be foreign to the Christian.

I heard a psychologist once say that there is one type of person who is relatively hopeless in counseling. That is the person who blames others for his or her problems. He indicated that such a person chooses to remain a victim.

It was Eleanor Roosevelt who observed, "No one can hurt you without your consent." Gandhi was a living example of this belief. A frail man wearing a loincloth and sandals almost single-handedly convinced the people of India to seek their independence from the British Commonwealth through peaceful means. Over and over again he reminded them, "They cannot take away our self-respect if we do not give it to them." He taught the people that no one could hurt them without their consent.

A second deadly attitude is self-pity. It is closely akin to the blame game in that it makes victims of its owners. Whereas blaming is aggressive, self-pity is passive; but both are deadly. Self-pity causes you to withdraw, internalize your hurts, and feel sorry for yourself.

There probably isn't a person alive who hasn't indulged in self-pity for at least a short period of time. If you wallow in it, however, it is like being pulled down in quicksand. It is a downward spiral that leads from self-pity to negativism, discouragement, despair, and depression. The theme song of people living in self-pity might be the silly little song some of us sang as children:

> Nobody loves me, everybody hates me,
> I'm going to the garden and eat worms.
> Big, fat juicy worms; long, slim slimey worms,
> I'm going to the garden and eat worms.

Are any of the three deadly attitudes—blaming others, self-pity, distrust/doubt—a part of my life? Which of these is keeping me from becoming the Christian I was called to be?

A third attitude to avoid is distrust and doubt. Honest doubt is good if you are seeking to know the truth, because it leads you to knowledge and faith. If, however, your doubt stems from a basic distrust of people, institutions, or God, you are in real trouble. This kind of doubt separates you from others, closes your mind to opportunities, and keeps you from the very resources you need.

When Jesus went to preach in his home village of Nazareth, he was met with doubt and distrust. The people could not imagine that one of their own could do what Jesus did. Both Matthew and Mark state flatly the results of the people's unwillingness to recognize Jesus' authority. Matthew says, "And he did not do many deeds of power there, because of their unbelief" (Matthew 13:57).

DREAMS CAN BECOME REALITIES

An illustration of how thoughts can be turned into dreams and beliefs is the story of Jesse Owens, who grew up in Cleveland, Ohio, in a home which he described as "materially poor, but spiritually rich." Charlie Paddock, a great athlete and one often described as "the fastest human being alive," came to speak at Jesse's school. He said to the kids, "Listen! What do you think you would like to be when you grow up? You name it, hold on to that thought until it becomes a dream, and believe that God will help you be that."

Am I missing God's dream because my life is like a ship covered with barnacles and not seaworthy for life's ocean? Are some of those barnacles listed in this chapter?

Young Jesse Owens thought to himself, "I want to be what Mr. Paddock has been. I want to be the fastest human being on earth." Rushing from the auditorium to the gymnasium, he said exuberantly to his coach, "I have a dream! I have a dream!" The coach replied, "It is great to have a dream, Jesse, but you have to build a ladder to your dreams, and the first rung on your ladder is attitude.

The second is determination, third is discipline, and the fourth is dedication." The result of Jesse Owens's thoughts, dreams, attitudes, and beliefs are well known. He was the fastest man ever to run the 100 meter dash and the 200 meter dash. His broad jump record lasted for twenty-four years. He won four gold medals in the Berlin Olympic Games. And his name was included in the charter list of the American Hall of Athletic Fame.

We, too, should remember that we are becoming what we think about. Thoughts are powerful because they determine attitudes, beliefs, and character. Jesus summarized it succinctly when He said: "All things can be done for one who believes" (Mark 9:23).

EXERCISES FOR DEVELOPING BETTER ATTITUDES

1. Recognizing that attitudes come from thoughts, begin to monitor your thought patterns:

⁂ For one day, write down all your negative thoughts. Realizing that negative thoughts, like dead weight, pull you down, go for one full day without a negative thought. Intercept it and replace it with a positive thought. Don't be afraid of becoming a Pollyanna. You are seeking to break destructive patterns and to become positive because you truly believe that Jesus Christ is Lord.

⁂ Use this scripture as an affirmation and reminder: "Whatever is true, whatever is honorable, whatever is just, whatever is pure, whatever is pleasing, whatever is commendable, if there is any excellence or if there is anything worthy of praise, think about these things" (Philippians 4:8).

2. Think of the person you criticize most often. Try to put yourself into his or her shoes. Remember how Jesus affirmed people through encouragement rather than criticism.

3. Develop the attitude of gratitude by practicing it. Express appreciation to family and friends, and write thank-you notes to people who are making your community a better place. Early each morning condition your mind with gratitude and express it as thanksgiving to God.

4. Seek to perform one act of kindness each day without any thought of return. This will sensitize you to feeling compassion for others.

CHAPTER SIX

Mental Termites at Work

*O*ur minds are like giant computers, and as the computer experts say, "Garbage in, garbage out." Pollution of the environment is a terrible thing, but pollution of the mind is even worse. Though we usually think of mind pollution as consisting of evil, violent, murderous, or pornographic thoughts, we can also pollute our minds with negative, fearful, resentful, and jealous thoughts. These thoughts are like little termites or saboteurs that destroy the tranquillity of our minds and spirits.

Have you ever had trouble with termites? They are devious little creatures that will undermine your house while you walk around under the false assumption that everything is okay.

A friend owned a house for less than a year when he discovered that the entire structure was ready to collapse because of termites. On the outside, the house looked great. It had just been painted before he purchased it. He also knew, from having lived in the same neighborhood, that the house had withstood a flood and a tornado. Yet, all the while it was subtly being destroyed by the small, mostly out-of-sight creatures that "worked without ceasing."

In a similar way, people often go through the crises of life with flying colors. They take time to mourn traumas and tragedies, but then move on constructively with their lives. Yet many of these same people all the while are being destroyed by the termites of negativism, fear, worry, anger, and resentment.

THE TERMITE OF NEGATIVISM

One of the most common mental termites is negativism. This isn't hard to understand since we are bombarded daily by the media with news of unrest, terrorism, and violence. If we choose to fill our minds with a steady diet of these kinds of thoughts, we fall prey to and become inundated by negativism. We become pessimistic, unhappy people.

Several years ago I was leading seminars for the Junior League in a distant city. The mother of one of the members invited me to stay over for a day and speak to the senior adults in her new church. When I entered the meeting room the following day, I was amazed at the evident vitality and energy, especially when the hostess told me that the average age of those present was eighty-six.

She sat me down beside a woman who was only in her early eighties. I began our conversation by saying, "Oh, I like your new church. It is so beautiful." Without so much as a smile, she replied curtly, "It's too big; it cost too much money; I wasn't in favor of building it." Realizing that I should try a different approach and thinking the weather would be safe, I asked, "Haven't we been having lovely weather this week?" Still without a smile, she replied, "Yes, but it snowed six times last winter, and every time it snowed I had the flu." Every time I said anything, she said, "Yes, but . . ."

Finally, my hostess rescued me and took me to the head table, saying: "I sat you down by Mrs. Jones because she is so negative, and I thought you might help her." Wearily, I replied, "If you had left me with her five more minutes, I couldn't have spoken." I was feeling so discouraged and depressed. The negative woman had created a climate of doom. Negative, pessimistic people infect others with their heavy gloom.

What about you? Is there anyone who hopes they don't see you in the morning until they have had a good strong cup of coffee?

In contrast, I have a delightful friend who is adept at changing a dismal conversation into a positive, fun experience. She is like a thermostat that actually changes the climate of a conversational group rather than a thermometer that simply reflects it. I was surprised to learn that in her early years of marriage, she had been a whining complainer who always expected the worst to happen.

"How did you change such a long-established negative pattern?" I once asked her. "Through a series of providences," she replied. "Before I became a Christian, I would have called them coincidences. Now I believe that it was the providence of God that led me from darkness into the light." She went on to tell me this story.

One Saturday evening after a full day of listening to my whining and pessimistic criticism, my husband sat me down, looked me straight in the eye and said, "Dorothy, I love you very much, but you are turning our home into a funeral parlor. I am already to the place that when I am tired I don't want to come home. Your negativism makes me feel as if I am walking into the valley of gloom." Immediately, I protested and told my husband that he was wrong. Very kindly he replied, "I'm convinced that deep down you are not a critical person and that the pressures of marriage and parenting have caused you to resort to early conditioning, so I have taped much of today's conversation so that you can hear for yourself."

Well, I listened in stunned disbelief to the recorded voice of a whining, complaining woman. It couldn't be mine! Yet, I knew I had said those very words. Suddenly I burst into tears and ran from the room. I was hurt, and I was angry with my husband. But stronger than the hurt was the sure knowledge that I was at a crisis point in my life and marriage. I fell to my knees and prayed, "Oh God, I am so confused. Help me to know who I am and what you want me to be."

In less than a week my prayer was beginning to be answered in a rather dramatic fashion. That very evening after my husband and I had a wonderful experience sharing our feelings, I remembered an article I had read about an organization called

"The Christophers." Their motto flashed across my mind: "It is better to light one candle than to curse the darkness."

That's it, I thought. I need to seek light rather than darkness. I diligently marked all of the passages in the Bible having to do with light. For example, Jesus told us to be the light of the world, not just to reflect light. There was only one way to "be light," and that was to stay close to the source—hence, a disciplined renewal of my faith.

Also, during that week we had a minister of counseling join the staff of our church. That man of God has helped me to erase early negative conditioning. So, you see, my prayer was answered.

Negativism for many people is a thought pattern that has become habitual. You may have been reared in a negative environment where you were negatively conditioned by parents or other authority figures, but you can interrupt the pattern. It will take time and effort and prayer, but you can rid your mind of the pollutant of negativism. You can become a thermostat instead of a thermometer. There is a "more-so" philosophy at work in life. Whatever you are now, you will, through the power of habit, become *more so* as you grow older. That is, unless you interrupt the pattern.

If you are negative now, you will be more so when you get old. If you are a bore at twenty, you will be an unbearable bore at seventy; if you are stingy at eighteen, you'll be a terrible tightwad at sixty. Sometimes in speaking to a mixed audience, I say, "Women, there is nothing in the world worse than an old woman who is mean, petty, whining, and complaining, unless it is an old man who is mean, petty, whining, and complaining. Both are the crowning works of the devil!"

Yet the opposite is also true. If you are friendly, outgoing, gracious, and caring, you will become more so as you add years to your life. The secret, of course, is to make some changes.

When I went through a very stressful period of my life, I found myself reverting to negative conditioning. In addition to prayer, two simple techniques helped me tremendously. First, I learned to interrupt the thought pattern. For example, if I had a negative thought such as, "I'll never get this finished. I'm overwhelmed," I would interrupt the pattern. Then I would say to myself: "Of course I can finish this. I have all the time and ability necessary to do it. I will organize and attack one small part of the problem each day."

The second thing I did was to wear a rubber band around my wrist. When I said or thought anything negative, I would snap the rubber band against my wrist. It hurt! When you do that fifty or seventy-five times a day, it really hurts! But it also makes you think twice before entertaining a negative thought.

After all, negativism begins a downward spiral into discouragement, despair, and depression. Remember that ships don't come in to shore on rough waters. If you want to think clearly, creatively, and concisely about a problem, you need to prepare your mind with calm serenity and positive possibilities. Centuries ago, Paul understood this when he wrote, "Let the same mind be in you that was in Christ Jesus" (Philippians 2:5).

THE TERMITE OF FEAR

Perhaps nothing can immobilize you more readily than fear, which gnaws away at your inner being. Fear of failure causes you to sit on the sidelines of life when you could be out on the playing field using your talents in making a difference in the world. Fear of rejection keeps you from offering friendliness and hospitality. Fear of success keeps you locked in a comfortable but tedious job when you have the opportunity for a new challenge.

A favorite story of mine concerns the pilot of a 747 jetliner. As the plane taxied down the runway, the pilot's voice could be heard on the loudspeaker: "Good morning, ladies and gentlemen. Welcome aboard flight 827 en route to London's Heathrow Airport. We will reach a crusing altitude of 30,000 feet and will be traveling at a speed of 350 miles per hour. Our flight time will be six hours. We will fly over Canada, Greenland, Iceland, and the tip of Ireland. As soon as we reach our cruising altitude, the flight attendants will serve you breakfast. We will take off . . . as soon as I get up my nerve."

Haven't we all felt like that pilot at times? But only fools are completely fearless. There are normal and healthy fears, and there are abnormal fears. A healthy fear of water, for example, motivates you to learn to swim and to practice water safety. A healthy fear of fire motivates you to install fire alarms and sprinkler systems. Abnormal fears, however, paralyze you, making it impossible to take actions that need to be taken.

There is a legend of a peasant who was riding into a medieval city and stopped to offer a ride to a stranger. The stranger introduced himself as Cholera and said he was going into the city to kill people by the plague. When the peasant expressed horror, Cholera said, "I'm only going to kill ten people. Here, I will leave you my dagger, and if I kill more than ten, you can kill me on my return." More than 100 persons died from the plague. Incensed, the peasant drew his dagger to kill Cholera when he returned. "Wait a minute, my friend," said Cholera, "I kept my word. I killed only ten; the others died of fear."

Overcoming Fear

What can you do if you are victimized by fear? First, you can fight your fears. Remember that fears are thoughts, and you can change your thought patterns. If the fears are deep seated, you may need the help of a counselor to discover their roots. Also, you can fight your fears through prayer. As you go into prayer, prepare to receive God's peace by using the following affirmations:

The LORD is my light and my salvation;
　　whom shall I fear?
The LORD is the stronghold of my life;
　　of whom shall I be afraid? (Psalm 27:1-2)
In God I trust; I will not be afraid.
　　What can a mere mortal do to me? (Psalm 56:11)
There is no fear in love, but perfect love casts out fear. (I John 4:18)

Second, despite your fears, you need, with the help of God, to act courageously. Teddy Roosevelt is reported to have said, "I have often been afraid, but I wouldn't give in to it. I have made myself act as if I were not afraid and gradually the fear disappeared." Likewise, Emerson reminded us, "Do the thing you fear and the death of fear is certain." Rather than fretting about our fears, we need to take positive action to overcome them.

The late William James, professor at Harvard University, suggested an "act as if" philosophy. He said that most people act on their feelings. For example, if a person awakens feeling "ornery," he or she will act "ornery" all day. James suggested that a person should decide how he or she is going to act (based on the Christian faith), act that way, and the feelings will follow. As Shakespeare said, "Assume a virtue until you have it." In other words, if you don't feel very confident, act with confidence until it becomes a part of your very nature.

This certainly should be true for Christians. The Christian faith is not based on feelings but on the fact that God loves us. John Wesley counseled his lay preachers to preach faith until they had it and then to preach faith *because* they had it.

This principle was vividly illustrated for me when our younger son came home from college for the summer. He had a summer job with a construction crew. It was hard, hot work, and he usually came home exhausted. His chore at home was to mow the lawn. How well I remember one Monday morning when his father reminded him that the lawn had to be mowed by Friday. "Yes sir," replied our son.

On Monday, Tuesday, and Wednesday he returned home too tired to mow the lawn. Late Thursday afternoon he told me that he had worked in 100 degree temperature in the blazing sun all day. Obviously that was not the day to mow the lawn. On Friday morning, my husband reminded our son again that this was the day.

In the late afternoon, our son returned home drenched with perspiration but went immediately to get our hand-pushed lawn mower. As I watched him, I decided he was moving more like a ninety-year-old man than a junior in college. That is, until his girlfriend, who had been away in summer school, stopped by and asked him to go play tennis. He finished that lawn in no time flat, came in, and showered before they went to play tennis. Later he returned to shower and dress again before they went out to dinner. Did he rest in so short a time? No. He changed his thoughts. He "acted as if."

Seeing such a vivid demonstration of this philosophy, I decided to try it myself. In the past when I couldn't sleep well, my mental conversation would go something like this: "Oh, my goodness, it is midnight and I have to get up at 6:00 A.M.; I'll be dead tomorrow!" Then at 2:00 A.M., I would exclaim, "Only four more hours; I'll be a zombie!" The following morning I would drag myself out of bed, and with a total lack of energy or enthusiasm, I would dress and walk dispiritedly into the office. There I would greet my colleagues with: "Did you know that I got only four hours sleep last night?" I discovered first, that people don't care how tired you are and, second, that just talking about it makes you more fatigued.

The next time my sleeplessness occurred, I decided to "act as if." The following morning I hopped out of bed, showered, and dressed quickly. After a good breakfast I drove to work and walked into the office with an energetic step. I never mentioned my sleeplessness to anyone. It was amazing how quickly my thoughts followed my actions. I began to feel energized.

The same thing applies to overcoming fear. You need to remind yourself that God does not intend for you to be a victim of fear. In II Timothy 1:7 we read: "For God did not give us a spirit of cowardice, but rather a spirit of power and of love and self-discipline."

> **Am I paralyzed by fear? (Practice exercise 3 regularly. See page 81.)**

The strongest way to battle fear is to build up faith. When I began to speak publicly I was terrified. My knees shook, my voice quivered, my palms perspired, and my throat got dry.

One of the things that helped me most (in addition to continuing to speak) was to repeat silently, before I began, the following powerful affirmation from Philippians 4:13: "I can do all things through him who strengthens me." This scriptural affirmation calmed my spirit by reminding me that I was not alone. I was empowered by the presence of Christ. The truth we all need to learn is that we don't have to be victimized by fear. We can overcome fear.

THE TERMITE OF WORRY

Worry is another mental termite. This negative emotion keeps you in inner turmoil, using up energies that could be used for happy, constructive living.

The Anglo-Saxon root word for *worry* means "to strangle." If you have ever been really worried about something, you know how right on target that meaning is. You feel as if you can't breathe. "I'm worried sick" is another apt description. Worry is the misuse of imagination.

My Aunt Vera was the worst worrier I have ever encountered. To be around her was to be robbed of any vestige of joy. She was always worried that she was about to come down with some dreaded disease. When she came to visit us, the windows couldn't be left open because she might be in a draft and catch cold. She couldn't go to the church picnic with us because people and flies would be there, and they both carry germs. When she died at an old age of natural causes, I am sure she would have liked her epitaph to read, "I told you I was sick."

Mark Twain said that he had known a lot of troubles in his life and most of them had never happened. I remember reading about a businessman who decided to analyze his worries. He said that 40 percent of them were likely

What do my worries reveal about the priorities in my life?

never to happen; 30 percent were about situations in the past that couldn't be changed; 12 percent concerned criticism from others (which he said didn't really matter); 10 percent of the worries were about his health (which he was already doing his best to protect); so only 8 percent were legitimate causes of worry. Analyze your worries and see if you are using your energies on past or imagined events.

Maxie Dunnam, in his workbook *How to Cope as Christians* says, "Worry is negative and concern is positive." Worry is like a broken record. Your thoughts go round and round in the same groove, and you can't get unstuck for action. Concern, on the other hand, is seeing the same problem from a clear perspective and then taking positive action to correct it. If you can't do anything about it, you need to turn it loose.

THE TERMITE OF UNCONTROLLED ANGER

Uncontrolled anger spoils friendships, destroys marriages, alienates parents and children, and costs many people their jobs. To be angry is not wrong, but to express anger destructively is wrong. When you lose your temper because you are out of control, you are less than God intended you to be. In Proverbs 16:32, we read,

> One that is slow to anger is better than the mighty,
> and one whose temper is controlled than one who
> captures a city.

The Bible also instructs us, "Be angry but do not sin" (Ephesians 4:26).

Anger is like steam—if it is to have constructive value, it must be under control. Steam can be used to blow a horn and make a lot of noise, or it can be used to turn the wheels of a steam locomotive. People are like that. It is easy to use up your anger over any little thing that happens—when you are inconvenienced, when your feelings are hurt, when you aren't recognized enough, and so forth. As a result, you have no anger left to put under God's control to change the evils of the world. When Jesus became angry and drove the money changers out of the Temple (Luke 19:45-46), he was not acting out of personal hurt but out of a desire to change an evil system.

The feelings of anger may be the motivation you need to make a difference in the world. If Abraham Lincoln hadn't become incensed about the evils of slavery, we may never have had the Emancipation Proclamation. If Robert Raikes hadn't felt anger about the children of England who had no opportunity to learn, we may never have had Sunday schools.

On the other hand, uncontrolled anger is a loss of control—"blowing up" in anger or seriously endangering a relationship with a spouse, a child, a parent, a friend, or a colleague.

I remember, as if a neon sign were calling my attention to it, the day I lost control with one of our children over a minor misdemeanor but one that had imposed great inconvenience on me. As I said some harsh, unkind words I suddenly saw the look of deep hurt in our son's eyes. I stopped in midsentence, asked forgiveness for my explosion and explained why the misdemeanor must not be repeated. Then, I made a hasty retreat to our bedroom where I dropped to my knees and asked God for forgiveness and for help in controlling my anger.

Am I using my anger in constructive or destructive ways? What are some healthy methods of venting my anger?

In my own case, I began to see other destructive patterns that fed my anger and needed to be dealt with for my own spiritual and emotional health, as well as for my relationships. Patterns such as perfectionism, self-centeredness, and paralyzing fear began to surface. Even the source of some of my pent up rage became evident— my father's alcoholism at a very vulnerable time in my life.

Obviously, all of this didn't happen in one session with God. My desire and decision to change were reinforced by an honest look at my life and relationships, a disciplined prayer life in which I honestly sought guidance, wide reading in the area of Christian living, and keeping a spiritual journal. In these ways we can stay in touch with our spiritual core in this noisy, fast-paced, technological world.

THE TERMITE OF RESENTMENT

Resentment, a feeling of indignation over perceived hurts and offenses, is like a splinter that gets under your skin. If it isn't removed, it produces infection.

Recently when I was presenting some seminars at a bank in Georgia, one of the employees who came to talk with me was a thirty-nine-year-old secretary. I noticed the lines of tension in her face and her posture of despair.

Ostensibly, she came to talk to me about her feeling of being left out of office conversation and camaraderie. As we talked, she spoke of recurring headaches, insomnia, and stomach problems. Discovering that she had just had a complete physical checkup, I began to probe about what really was bothering her. It turned out that she was harboring a grudge against her sister, whom she believed had manipulated her parents. The sister received a little more of the family inheritance than she did.

The incident had happened twenty years earlier, and the accumulated weight of carrying such a grudge was evident in her bitter spirit, her physical symptoms, and her bad interpersonal relationships. She was not hurting her sister by her reactions, but she was destroying herself.

Her only way out was to forgive her sister and close the door on the past. Her resistance to the suggestion was obvious. I'm afraid that she chose to hold on to the grudge, either because it was habitual or because she felt justified in her resentment. She chose to do this, even though she was, and maybe still is, paying a terrible physical and emotional price—and even though she could be free any day of her choosing. In Mark 11:25 Jesus tells us, "Whenever you stand praying, forgive, if you have anything against anyone; so that your Father in heaven may also forgive you your trespasses."

Am I holding a grudge against anyone?
How has this grudge affected my physical,
emotional, and spiritual well-being?

When you feel justified in your resentment, it is easy and comfortable to hold on to it. But it is deadly! As a splinter under your skin can cause infection unless removed, so resentment in your spirit can cause bitterness, anger, cynicism, and loss of enthusiasm and joy.

Sometimes when you face your resentments, you may have to initiate a "care-frontation" in which you seek reconciliation. Sometimes you may need to ask for forgiveness and make restitution. Sometimes you just may have to decide to move on with your life—to take your life off hold.

GETTING RID OF MENTAL TERMITES

Whether the termite is negativism, fear, worry, anger, resentment, or some other emotion, many people choose to hold on to the destructive emotion. I once read about an expedition of scientists who were on a mission to capture a particular species of monkeys in the jungles of Africa. It was important that the monkey be brought back alive and unharmed. Using their knowledge of monkey ways, the scientists designed a trap consisting of a jar with a long neck. Into the jar was placed a handful of nuts. Smelling the nuts, a monkey would thrust his paw into the long neck and take a fistful of nuts. But when he tried to withdraw the prize, he discovered that his clenched fist would not pass through the narrow neck of the bottle. So, he was trapped in the anchored bottle, unable to escape with his booty, and yet unwilling to let it go. Often we too cling to the very things that hold us back, remaining captive because of our sheer unwillingness to let go.

What can we do to get unstuck and move on with our lives? How can we bring serenity and balance to our hectic lives? First, we can prune our activities and simplify our life-styles. More and more I am convinced that we spend time, energy, and the big part of our lives securing things that we don't need and can little enjoy because we are so busy working to pay for and maintain them. Letting go of these unnecessary complications and distractions frees us of preoccupation with worry, stress, and debilitating fatigue.

I have learned that I can cast off my preoccupation with worry by quiet affirmation of Scripture passages. These have helped me: "Cast all your anxiety on him, because he cares for you" (I Peter 5:7); "Those of steadfast mind you keep in peace— / in peace because they trust in you" (Isaiah 26:3).

Also, we can learn to live one day at a time, rather than dragging yesterday and tomorrow into today. Sir William Osler, who organized the Johns Hopkins School of Medicine, urged the students at Yale University, where he lectured, to live in day-tight compartments. He reminded them of the petition in the Lord's Prayer: "Give us this day our daily bread." This gives us the ability to focus, to take advantage of today's opportunities, and to celebrate life.

In addition, we can practice forgiveness and take time for silence and prayer. Effective prayer is not an extended worry session (recounting all our problems), even if it begins with "Our Father" and ends with "Amen." And it is not just a "give me" prayer. Prayer that brings power for living also includes silence, when we are open to God and to his direction. When our minds are calm and our spirits are open to God, he can communicate with us through new and creative ideas. He can also provide direction as he calls to our remembrance helpful Scripture passages.

Edwin Markham wrote, "At the heart of the cyclone, tearing the sky, is a place of central calm." If we are to live with power and poise in a hectic world, we must learn to be receivers as well as achievers. Spiritual freedom is an inside job.

EXERCISES FOR OVERCOMING NEGATIVE EMOTIONS

1. For one week, write down all your negative thoughts. It may surprise you how polluted your mind has become. Then, through a prayerful act of the will, begin to interrupt each negative thought and expression with a positive but honest thought. Also, try the rubber band technique (see page 71). It is a technique that worked for me.

If your negativism is deep seated and you find yourself depressed regularly, you may need to talk with a Christian counselor. Sometimes hurts and fears that we experienced early in life need to be resolved before we can move on in positive hope.

2. Write your greatest fear and face it. If the absolute worst thing that could happen to you actually happened, how would you and God handle it? Write a plan of action to give yourself a sense of control. Remember that with God all things are possible.

3. Faith is the antidote for fear. Make time for private and corporate worship, for talking and listening to God in prayer, and for reading the Bible regularly—particularly those passages that deal with faith. For example: "If you have faith the size of a mustard seed, you will say to this mountain, 'Move from here to there,' and it will move; and nothing will be impossible for you" (Matthew 17:20). "For we walk by faith, not by sight" (II Corinthians 5:7). "Jesus said to him, 'If you are able!—All things can be done for the one who believes'" (Mark 9:23).

Absorb these passages in your mind. Use them as powerful affirmations when you are fearful. Remember: "God did not give us a spirit of cowardice, but rather a spirit of power and of love and of self-discipline" (II Timothy 1:7).

4. Keep a spiritual journal in which you record your feelings, struggles, hopes, and dreams. You will begin to see an emerging picture of who you are and how God can help you become what you were meant to be.

5. Each day in a quiet time of prayer, release any fears, worries, resentments, or grudges you may have. Confess these to God and ask his forgiveness. Consider what steps you need to take to overcome them. Sometimes, this is simply letting go of them.

CHAPTER SEVEN

Live with Optimism

Are you an optimist or a pessimist? Is your approach to life—the window through which you view the world—something you are born with or is it learned?

For most of my own life I believed that one's outlook on life comes as standard equipment. If you are born with the genes for a happy, sunny temperament, then you are an optimist. If, on the other hand, you are born with the genes for a melancholic, sensitive, introverted temperament, you see the world through pessimistic eyes.

Determinism is the belief that our lives are determined by things beyond our control. Genetic determinism places the blame on heredity—"your grandparents did it to you." Unfortunately, far too many people share this misguided belief. Whether intentionally or unintentionally, they excuse every character and personality flaw—bad temper, lying, inaptitude for certain academic subjects—on genes. For example, I knew a girl in college who didn't like mathmatics and avoided all math courses she could by saying, "I have deficient math genes."

Am I selling my Christian heritage short by getting discouraged too easily? Do I give in to depression without an attempt to change my thought pattern?

Psychological determinism blames one's upbringing—"the way you are brought up and trained by your parents determines who you are." Environmental determinism says that we are determined by environment—one's boss, spouse, teenager, economic situation, or national politics.

Obviously, all of these factors influence us, but as Christians we know that God endowed us with wonderful, human capabilities that lift us above the stimulus and response level. These capabilities include self-awareness, imagination, conscience, and independent will. They give us the freedom to choose and make us "a little lower than the angels and crown us with honor and glory" (Psalm 8:5 Author's Paraphrase).

Austrian psychriatrist Viktor Frankl learned and reported in his book *Man's Search for Meaning* that even in the degrading, repugnant, inhumane conditions of a Nazi concentration camp, he had the freedom to choose his reactions. He called this our ultimate, God-given freedom. What happens to us is not nearly as important as how we react to what happens.

As Christians, we have only to look at how Jesus faced life's tragedies, even death on the cross, and used them for good and for the glory of God. Likewise, Paul took difficulties and defeats and turned them into vital victories because his hope, his trust, and his very life were rooted in faith in Christ. Only then could he write, "All things work together for good for those who love God, who are called according to his purpose" (Romans 8:28).

Am I guilty of "locked-in" thinking? Are my thought patterns the result of deeply held beliefs or are they simply habitual?

Optimism for the Christian is based on a faith that nothing can happen that we and God together cannot handle. This doesn't mean being unrealistic or putting our heads in the sand or expecting no difficulties. It means that because of our belief in God, in Christ, and in the power of the Holy Spirit, we believe in ourselves and feel competent to face life. We know that difficulties will come, but we see them as temporary and as challenges rather than problems. "In the world you face persecution. But take courage; I have conquered the world" (John 16:33).

LEARNED OPTIMISM

In the past three decades, the findings of outstanding psychiatrists, psychologists, and sociologists have helped us understand that optimism and pessimism are learned. For example, psychiatrist Aaron T. Beck and psychologist Albert Ellis challenged long-held views about depression. They argued that depression is not a result of brain chemistry or anger turned inward, but rather a disorder of conscious thought. In other words, depressed people need to be helped to change wrong thinking into right thinking.

Perhaps the person who has made this concept most understandable is Martin E. P. Seligman, Professor of Psychiatry at the University of Pennsylvania. He is the leading authority on "learned helplessness" (pessimism), "learned optimism," and what he calls "explanatory style," or what you say to yourself when you experience setbacks. In his book *Learned Optimism,* Seligman suggests that optimism or its opposite, pessimism, is learned basically from your primary caregiver (usually mother) in the first seven years of life. However, if you have been programmed by a pessimistic parent or a significant other, you can change the programming. (The steps in this process will be discussed later in this chapter.)

Do I need to become more flexible as a person by looking for alternate solutions?

Changing negative programming is important because optimism is so powerful. Optimism provides bounce-back ability and enables you to see problems as possibilities, to keep yourself motivated and energized, and to build a positive *esprit de corps* in family, job, or other team relationships. Recent studies indicate that optimists excel in their work, have better health, establish long and happy marriages, stay connected to their children, and perhaps even live longer.

For the Christian, the source of optimism is the joyful knowledge that we are loved and forgiven by God. When we accept this gift of love, made evident to us through the death of Jesus ("For God so loved the world that he gave his only Son, so that everyone who believes in him may not perish but may have eternal life" John 3:16), we are empowered for living in the here and now.

Let's look at the characteristics of an optimist and ask how we can incorporate these into our lives.

CHARACTERISTICS OF AN OPTIMIST

From my observation and wide reading on the subject of optimism, I believe that optimists have the following characteristics.

1. Optimists are not rigid in their approach to life. They are flexible enough to look for alternate solutions to problems.

2. Optimists are willing to tackle big projects or problems by working on one segment or one part at a given time. For example, if cleaning a large garage seems an impossible task, they clean one corner and move on to the next without feeling overwhelmed.

3. Optimists are "can-do" people who believe that problems have solutions.

4. Optimists believe they have a great deal of control over circumstances. They understand and don't fret over the fact that some things cannot be changed, but they change what can be changed.

5. Optimists have generally learned to control their thoughts and to interrupt negative thought patterns.

6. Optimists practice the art of being cheerful.

7. Optimists have learned the art of renewing and energizing themselves.

8. Optimists have good interpersonal relationships and consequently a network of support. They have a desire to continue growing toward wholeness.

9. Optimists are grounded in a strong value system. For Christians, this is based on a bedrock faith in Jesus Christ.

These characteristics are important because they allow us to live in a stressful, negative, and often evil world without being overcome by evil or losing hope. It reminds us that "The one who is in you is greater than the one who is in the world" (I John 4:4).

OPTIMISM HELPS WHEN YOU ARE ILL

Optimism is an important outlook for every day of life, but it is especially helpful in times of illness. I learned this in a very personal way just a year ago. My husband and I were conducting a seminar at a church that was one hundred miles from our home. On Saturday evening as I dressed to go to the church, I felt something hard in my abdomen. Though it caused me slight concern, I decided it was hardened muscle resulting from increased abdominal exercise.

Four months earlier my dress size had increased by one size because of what I thought was the "middle-age" spread from a more sedentary life-style. Knowing that I must do something about this, I greatly increased my morning calisthenics with special concentration on abdominal exercises. That Saturday night, I assumed that I had a hardened abdominal muscle and didn't even mention this to my husband.

Around 2:00 A.M. on the following day I awakened with my fears as thick as flies at an outdoor summer picnic. "What if this is not a hardened muscle? What if it is a tumor? What if it is malignant? What if I die?" Those terrifying thoughts gave me a panic attack. Then, Scripture (as it has done so often in the past) brought me back to the source of my optimism—God's love and grace as seen in his promises and made evident in the person of Jesus Christ.

My mind went immediately to a verse that a college class-mate shared with me when several people close to me had died. In college that scriptural affirmation enabled me to move from fear to faith, and now years later, I found it doing the same thing. God's promise in Psalm 89:33 became a powerful aid in allowing me to stay optimistic: "Nevertheless [whatever happens] my loving kindness I will not take from you and my faithfulness will not fail you" (KJV).

Upon returning home, I immediately set up an appointment with an internist. Through various tests she determined that I had a large abdominal cyst, and she scheduled an appointment for me with the surgeon of my choice. The surgery was performed three days later. There was a malignancy, and the surgery was followed by eight months of chemotherapy. Throughout the entire experience that Bible verse (Psalm 89:33) helped me to move from fear to faith.

Another means of keeping optimism alive in difficult circumstances is to recall and affirm some deeply held beliefs. For example, I have always believed that opportunities and joys lie hidden within problems and difficulties. After surgery when I awakened in the intensive care unit, I discovered tubes coming from every part of my body. I found myself thinking, "Okay, Nell, where are the opportunities in this experience?" Well, I found a few of them that day and more with each passing day.

That day I began to feel an overwhelming sense of joy at being surrounded by my family and friends. Though I never saw them during the day of surgery, I was fully aware that twenty of my friends spent the five hours of my operation—7:00 A.M. until noon—in the hospital chapel talking to the Great Physician on my behalf. Since then I have often felt a great surge of joy for the love and commitment of these friends who would give up five hours of their Saturday morning to pray for me. In addition, so many other people who read my weekly column wrote that they were praying for me. In fact, one person wrote, "Only the troops in the Persian Gulf have had more people praying for them than you had." It was wonderful to have the assurance that "underneath are the Everlasting arms."

During the first week of hospitalization, I became acutely aware of the healing presence of friends—particularly, cheery, optimistic ones. I still laugh about the day when nurses were having to bring in extra tables for arriving flower arrangements. In the midst of the activity, my internist walked in. In an offhand manner she declared, "My goodness, the florist must be having a sale on flowers!"

Norman Cousins was right on target when he spoke of the therapeutic value of laughter. A remark such as my doctor's, spoken when I was in pain and was experiencing numerous indignities—such as a tube in my nose that irritated my throat and made me sound like Donald Duck!—is like finding water in the desert. Delightful!

Staying optimistic allowed me to focus on the joys rather than the difficulties of the situation. Though ours has always been a close family, we became even closer during this experience. We talked about things most families don't take time to talk about in the pressures of everyday living. We spoke of eternal things, of the meaning of life and death, of our dreams for the future, and of how much we mean to one another. Our son and his wife made time in their demanding schedule of work and child rearing to "be there" for me. My husband deserves a special medal as "nurse of the year." Following surgery, he spent each night, except one when he was away on business, at the hospital as well as returning with me each month for the overnight chemotherapy treatments. He was the one who provided cold cloths and soothing words during my bouts with nausea.

Do I have a tendency to get overly stressed or burned out when pursuing a project at work or at home? Do I need to practice the art of personal renewal?

Most of all, God's presence was very real to me. God's presence gave me strength to "hang in there"; he gave me comfort when I grew weary and he gave me guidance—such as the idea of cooperating with instead of fighting chemotherapy.

In addition, God gave me wonderful serendipities along the way. I am sure he does that constantly, but we often can't see them because we are so focused on the difficulty. When I awakened from surgery I was surrounded by my husband, our son, and my competent, caring surgeon. After giving me the facts—the large tumor (about the size of a small football) was malignant—he then spoke optimistically. The malignancy seemed to be contained within the tumor. With its removal and a series of eight to ten chemotherapy treatments, I should be "as good as new." That in itself was like a wonderful gift, but God added a big red bow in an immediate announcement made by our son: "Mother, I got a call for you this morning from Garden Grove, California, asking if you could speak at the International Women's Conference there in October." What a serendipity! It beckoned me beyond the long months of chemotherapy to an exciting opportunity.

CAN OPTIMISTS BE REALISTS?

Some people confuse being a Pollyanna with being an optimist. An authentic optimist is not one who just mindlessly repeats Emile Coue's, "Day by day in every way I'm getting better and better." Instead, the optimist weighs the facts and chooses to focus on the possibilities rather than the problems. Exercising their God-given wisdom, optimists discern the important issues and overlook the unimportant ones. It was William James who said, "The essence of genius is knowing what to overlook." The important

Do I need to strengthen my faith to allow me to see more of God's possibilities?

balance between tenacity and submission, between optimism and realism, was clarified graphically by W. C. Fields: "If at first you don't succeed, try once again. If the second time you don't succeed, try once again. But if the third time you don't succeed, quit. There is no use being a fool about it."

I am 5 feet 2 inches tall, but I would like to be at least 5 feet 6 inches tall. I, also, would like to have a good singing voice, but I don't. You have similar "unchangeables" in your life. A pessimist is one who goes through life whining, complaining, and fretting over the unchangeables. An authentic optimist is one who accepts what cannot be changed but does what he or she can to improve the situation. For example, I am short, but I can develop good posture so that I look taller, or I can wear high heels.

Christian optimists have bounce-back ability. They see the difficulties involved but determine to turn a bad situation into a higher good. Look at Paul and Silas in prison in Philippi. That was a bad situation, but they used it to serve God by singing hymns at midnight and converting the jailor (Acts 16:22-40). With God's help we, too, can find opportunities for a higher good in even the most difficult situations.

EXERCISES FOR BECOMING MORE OPTIMISTIC

1. When you awaken in the morning, condition your mind with gratitude. In the words of the hymn writer: "Count your many blessings, name them one by one. / And it will surprise you what the Lord hath done." This way you set the tone for your day.

2. Interrupt your negative thinking pattern. Learn to say "stop" when you begin exaggerating. When something bad happens, don't make the situation permanent ("diets never work"), universal ("all teachers are unfair"), or personal ("I'm stupid"). Avoid such words as *always, never,* and *all* that tend to make the situation seem hopeless. Step back and look clearly at the facts. (Remember the rubberband technique in chapter 6.)

3. Learn to look for alternate solutions. Recognize that it is easy to have "locked-in" thinking, and activate the right side of your brain by brainstorming. Ask yourself, "What are some possible solutions to this problem?" Then, write them down immediately no matter how farfetched they seem. A logical solution will begin to emerge.

4. Remember that all of us have daily work cycles—times when we are more creative, productive, and optimistic. Research indicates that mid to late morning and early evening are the most productive and optimistic times when we should do our critical thinking and work.

5. Practice believing and affirming the following: "Nothing can happen to me today that God and I together cannot handle"; "I can do all things through him who strengthens me" (Philippians 4:13); "If God be for us, who is against us?" (Romans 8:31); "We know that all things work together for good for those who love God, who are called according to his purpose" (Romans 8:28).

CHAPTER EIGHT

The Inside Story

You met Kathy in the first chapter of this book. She was the young woman who walked into the seminar room exuding warmth, friendship, and self-confidence. Everyone in the room felt drawn to her.

It is obvious that Jesus does not want us to be weak, ineffective, lethargic, or fearful persons. When he said, "I came that they may have life, and have it abundantly" (John 10:10), he implied that we are to live with confidence and power. He also gave us the key to becoming that kind of person: "But to all who received him, who believed in his name, he gave power to become the children of God."

This is the key that Kathy used in her growth toward wholeness. She wanted to know who she was and whose she was. Through her Sunday school teacher, she was helped to claim her Christian heritage. She understood that she was created in the image of God and is deeply loved by him. She has received God's forgiveness and acceptance, not by her own goodness or achievements, but by God's grace and the gift of himself in Jesus Christ. When she accepted this gift by receiving Christ into her life, she began to receive and assimilate his power for living.

As paradoxical as it may seem, we have to surrender our lives to the Lordship of Christ in order to be free and whole. Jesus gave us this paradox when he said: "Those who find their life will lose it, and those who lose their life for my sake will find it" (Matthew 10:39).

Have I found the freedom that comes from surrendering myself to the Lordship of Christ?

In surrender, the self does not die or become diminished. In fact, it is only then that we become fulfilled. When the self is of primary importance, it becomes what William James called "the convulsive little ego." This is true even when the self is "dressed up" to look like healthy ambition, righteous anger, or strong commitment. Instead of being integrated, the self-centered person becomes fragmented.

This was illustrated so graphically for me by a man who lived in the small town in which I grew up. He was the center of his universe. His conversations, his decisions, and his projects all centered around himself and his interests. He was a member of our church, and though he was very talented, no one wanted to work with him. If he were on a committee, he wanted to control all the decisions. If he didn't get his way, he withdrew financial support from the church. If he did get his way, most of the other committee members resigned because of this man's manipulation. He ended his life as a lonely, pathetic man without friends. He lost his life because he wasn't able to surrender it to something bigger than himself.

If we are honest, we know that this pull between self-centered living and Christ-centered living continues long after we come to faith. We must live in daily fellowship with Christ if we want to be integrated rather than fragmented. This pull toward fragmentation is expressed so well in Edward Sanford Martin's poem "Mixed":

> Within my earthly temple there's a crowd;
> There's one of us that's humble, one that's proud,
> There's one that's broken-hearted for his sins,
> There's one that unrepentant sits and grins;
> There's one who loves his neighbor as himself,
> And one that cares for naught but fame and pelf.
> From much corroding care I would be free
> If once I could determine which is me.

Only under the Lordship of Christ can the self be fully realized. It is then that we can tame the wild horses of passion and negative emotion, so that they work as servants rather than masters. In a strange way that we do not fully understand, the surrendered self becomes more aware of others, can live more harmoniously with them, and can live in deep communion with God. What a foundation for wholeness!

GROWTH IN SELF-CONFIDENCE

After you have accepted your Christian heritage and established your spiritual foundation, there are many things you can do to facilitate your growth in self-confidence. One well-known person who has exemplified this growth is Dr. Norman Vincent Peale.

Growing up as a minister's son in the small towns of Ohio, Dr. Peale was painfully shy and had a self-image of inadequacy. In an interview some years ago, Dr. Peale told me that he might have remained shy except for the intervention of a college professor. One day, after he had performed miserably in an oral presentation, his teacher asked him to stay after class. Without any tact or concern for the student's feelings, the professor blurted out: "How long are you going to act like a scared rabbit? You act as if you are afraid of the sound of your own voice! You had better change the way you think about yourself, Peale, before it is too late."

How honest and diligent have I been in seeking truly to know and understand myself? When I walk into a room, do I exude warmth, friendliness, and self-confidence? If not, what do I project?

Dr. Peale told me that he had become furious with the professor. Yet, he knew the man was right. Stronger than his anger was his desire to be whole. He began a plan of action that he has shared with millions of people through his books, tapes, and speeches. In the process he has become one of America's most popular lecturers, preachers, and writers.

A strongly confident person, one who accepts himself or herself as a person of worth, can accept others and relate to them without the need to control. Through many years of study, observation, and sometimes painful seeking, I have concluded that you cannot really love another until you are confident of who you are and have learned to exercise your unique gifts. You cannot really give yourself to another person until you have a self to give. When you are not threatened or intimidated by another person, you can reach out in acceptance and care enough for that person to be totally present.

> **Am I able to relate to the "significant others" in my life in accepting and caring ways?**

FREEDOM BY FAITH

Confident Christians know who they are and have been freed by their faith. It was the German philosopher Nietzsche who said, "He who has a 'why' to live for can bear almost any 'how'". On the Mount of Temptation, Jesus fully discovered the "why" of his living and was equipped for all the "hows"—even that of death on the cross. So it is that Christ frees us from meaninglessness. He gives us a purpose, a sense of mission, a feeling of self-worth, a basis for relationships, and a reason for being. He allows us to see the "whole" of life so that we can live in the mundane and the "nitty gritty" without disillusionment.

Christ also frees us from guilt. When we recognize our sins and repent of them, we are forgiven and restored to fellowship with Christ.

I once knew a man who could not forgive himself for not being at his wife's bedside when she died. He had been devoted to her throughout their twenty-five-year marriage, especially during the long months of her illness. He had hired nurses to be with her in their home while he was at work, but he usually took the night shift. Her last two weeks were spent in the hospital. Despite his fatigue, he spent each night with her.

On the twelfth day in the hospital, his wife seemed no worse than usual when he left for work that morning. He needed to be at his office to present a project for which he had major responsibility. The nurse, of course, had his office telephone number. But by midafternoon, his wife suddenly became worse, and she died before he could get to the hospital. In his anguish, he asked for and received God's forgiveness, but he could never forgive himself.

Today this man's life is on hold. He has been unable to hear God's call to move forward into the future. He desperately needs to hear Paul's words to the Galatians in what has been called the Magna Charta of spiritual freedom: "Christ has set us free. Stand firm, therefore, and do not submit again to a yoke of slavery" (Galatians 5:1).

The master key to self-confidence is found in the freedom offered by Christ on the cross. This is freedom from a fragmented self, from meaninglessness, from guilt and death. It frees us for creative living, for loving service, and for eternal life.

Nestled in the Great Smoky mountains there is a Christian assembly surrounded by a beautiful lake where multitudes of lives have been transformed, where romances have blossomed into love and marriage, and where many young people have made a commitment for full-time service in the church. Most of these decisions have been made at the foot of the lighted cross that stands high on a hill overlooking the lake. There is a story told about that lighted cross.

It seems that soon after the Great Depression began, the lighted cross was turned off at 10:00 P.M. in the summer months, and it was agreed by the assembly officials that the cross would not be turned on during the winter months. Then a conductor on the Southern Railway wrote a letter to the assembly officers saying, "Please don't turn off the cross. The men who work on my train derive much hope and comfort from the lighted cross when we make our nightly run through the mountains. Most of the men are fearful and anxious about their jobs and future, so please don't turn off the cross."

According to the story, the assembly officers decided to keep the cross lighted 365 nights a year. The railroad conductor's words have significance for each of us individually—"don't turn off the cross."

EXERCISES FOR BUILDING
SELF-CONFIDENCE

If you can fully accept yourself as a unique person who is created in the image of God, and if you have surrendered yourself to the Lordship of Christ, then it is possible to gain a healthy confidence in yourself. The following steps will help:

1. Focus on your strengths rather than on your weaknesses as you continue to overcome those weaknesses. Dr. Peale suggests that you stamp indelibly upon your mind a mental picture of yourself as an able and confident creation of God.

2. Even though it will require hard work, seek honestly to know and accept yourself. Be done with rationalizations and attempts to conform to others' expectations.

3. Determine to live above the fear of rejection and neurotic guilt.

4. Keep a clear picture in your mind of yourself living happily and successfully.

5. Replace fear of failure with positive affirmations such as: "I can do all things through him who strengthens me" (Philippians 4:13); "If God is for us, who is against us?" (Romans 8:31); "The one who began a good work among you will bring it to completion" (Philippians 1:6).

6. Distinguish *who you are* from *what you do.*

7. Find something you like to do and do well, and do it over and over again.

8. Dare to be different. If you have an inordinate need to please others, you will never be true to yourself. Don't try

to copy someone else. You will make a great original but a poor copy.

9. Insofar as possible, make peace with those persons who have wronged you.

10. Practice silence and relaxation daily for ten minutes (or for as long as you are able within your schedule).

11. Each night empty your mind of worries, fears, and resentments.

12. Cultivate friends who will help you grow.

13. Make a numerical estimate of your assets and raise it 10 percent. Most people tend to focus on their liabilities rather than their assets.

14. Make this a daily affirmation: "From this day on, with the help of God, I am becoming more and more conscious of all that is creative and positive. My life is becoming more Christ-centered, more efficient, and more effective."

A FINAL WORD

*I*t is my conviction that all Christians want to possess the abundant life of which Jesus spoke in John 10:10: "I came that they may have life, and have it abundantly." We know about our Christian heritage—made in the image of God, redeemed by Christ, and empowered by the Holy Spirit. That's a powerful image and heritage! Yet it is not easy to internalize that image in our thoughts, expectations, and attitudes and then live it out in our "nitty-gritty" everyday life.

We often interrupt the process of abundant living by continuing to foster a negative self-image. We also pollute our minds with fear, worry, anger, resentment, and other negative emotions.

It is my prayer that the practical suggestions given in this book will allow you to be the person God created you to be and to claim his promise of abundant living. In a nutshell, the formula for such living is found in Matthew 22:37-39: " 'You shall love the Lord your God with all your heart, and with all your soul, and with all your mind.' This is the greatest and first commandment. And a second is like it: 'You shall love your neighbor as yourself.' "

NOTES

NOTES